ROUTLEDGE LIBRARY EDITIONS: AGRIBUSINESS AND LAND USE

Volume 26

CREATING RURAL EMPLOYMENT

CREATING RURAL EMPLOYMENT

B. H. KINSEY

Routledge
Taylor & Francis Group

LONDON AND NEW YORK

First published in 1987 by Croom Helm Ltd.

This edition first published in 2024
by Routledge
4 Park Square, Milton Park, Abingdon, Oxon OX14 4RN

and by Routledge
605 Third Avenue, New York, NY 10158

Routledge is an imprint of the Taylor & Francis Group, an informa business

British Library Cataloguing in Publication Data
A catalogue record for this book is available from the British Library

ISBN: 978-1-032-48321-4 (Set)
ISBN: 978-1-032-47293-5 (Volume 26) (hbk)
ISBN: 978-1-032-47304-8 (Volume 26) (pbk)
ISBN: 978-1-003-38545-5 (Volume 26) (ebk)

DOI: 10.4324/9781003385455

Publisher's Note
The publisher has gone to great lengths to ensure the quality of this reprint but points out that some imperfections in the original copies may be apparent.

Disclaimer
The publisher has made every effort to trace copyright holders and would welcome correspondence from those they have been unable to trace.

Creating Rural Employment

B.H. KINSEY

CROOM HELM
London • Sydney • Wolfeboro, New Hampshire

© 1987 B.H. Kinsey
Croom Helm Ltd, Provident House, Burrell Row.
Beckenham, Kent, BR3 1AT

Croom Helm Australia Pty Ltd, Suite 4, 6th Floor,
64-76 Kippax Street, Surry Hills, NSW 2010, Australia

British Library Cataloguing in Publication Data
Kinsey, B.H.
    Creating rural employment.
    1. Manpower policy 2. Rural conditions
    I. Title
    331.12′042   HD5710.8
    ISBN 0-7099-1557-8

Croom Helm, 27 South Main Street,
Wolfeboro, New Hampshire 03894-2069, USA

Library of Congress Cataloging-in-Publication Data

Kinsey, B.H.
    Creating rural employment.

    Includes index.
    1. Manpower policy, Rural. 2. Public service
employment.   I. Title.   II. Title: Rural employment.
HD5710.8.K56   1987   331.12′042   86-16826
ISBN 0-7099-1557-8

Printed and bound in Great Britain by
Biddles Ltd, Guildford and King's Lynn

CONTENTS

Contents

Contents

TABLES AND FIGURES

Tables

Tables and Figures

Figures

For Elspeth

PREFACE

        The burgeoning growth of literature in economic
and social development since the early 1960s has
seen a remarkable number of short-lived fads as the
international agencies have directed funds first in
one and then in another direction attempting to
solve wide-reaching development problems through
relatively narrow interventions. One theme,
however, emerged early and has consistently been
given greater prominence with time: this is the
problem of creating productive employment in rural
areas where the majority of the population in developing countries now live and will continue to do so
for the foreseeable future. The importance of the
subject matter to which this manual is addressed has
therefore in no way diminished in the more than a
decade and a half since the authors began to study
rural public works--quite the contrary.

        High levels of unemployment are indicative of
extensive poverty with serious human, economic and
political dimensions. Government initiatives to
alleviate the problem of unemployment are essential.
Direct action to establish public sector employment-
creating programmes has been attempted in over 30
countries and is being considered by many more.
Rural public works programmes, however, require new
policies and forms of decentralised administrative
organisation which are novel in many situations. In
creating and implementing such programmes, potential
users of rural public works are therefore likely to
benefit considerably from the experience of other
countries.

        This manual is designed primarily for policy-
makers and programme administrators in those
countries considering or already implementing rural

public works programmes as a means of alleviating poverty. Its purpose is to organise the lessons of international experience with these programmes so that they can be applied effectively in a wide variety of circumstances. The manual attempts to establish realistically the potentials and limitations of rural public works programmes, to provide guidelines for deciding whether a programme can be effective in a particular area, to consider the major issues surrounding these programmes, to suggest organisational arrangements that will enhance their propects for success, and to provide criteria for judging their performance. Coupled with the local knowledge essential to good programme design, the compilation of experience and accumulated knowledge about this special type of development programme can be employed to benefit similar programmes in other countries.

The reference material in the earlier version of the manual has been supplemented with materials covering more recent experience and the experience of a wider range of countries than it was possible to cover in the manual. This broader set of comparative materials should prove useful in extending the application of the manual in a wide variety of circumstances.

B. H. Kinsey

ACKNOWLEDGEMENTS

This work is primarily a revision and updating of a reference manual prepared under contract for the United States Agency for International Development (USAID) by John Thomas and Richard Hook of the Harvard Institute for International Development. Peter Thorman of USAID served as project monitor and commentator, and Shahid Javed Burki and Richard Patten contributed useful ideas and concepts to that manual. The main audience for the original version was taken to be "policy makers and. programme administrators" in developing countries.

USAID has indicated that it supports the revision of this work because it "would promote development", and it is on this basis that the current version is authorised--and justified. Any errors or misjudgements in the revision remain, of course, the sole responsibility of the author.

In addition to the material from USAID, use has been made of the ILO/UNDP series of training courses on special public works programmes. Much recent field experience with rural works programmes has been supported by ILO, and current documentation relating this experience is listed at the end of this volume.

The author would like to express his appreciation to USAID for permission to publish the manual and to Iftikhar Ahmed of the International Labour Office for making available bibliographies of that organisation's recent research and experience with rural employment programmes. The production of the edited version of the manual was capably assisted by Sara Ahmed and Heather Latham.

Chapter One

INTRODUCTION

Unemployment is a major concern of people and governments in many countries around the world. [1] High levels of unemployment signify the existence of serious poverty that presents problems that are primarily human but have serious economic and political implications which require remedial action. Government initiatives to alleviate the problem are essential. Such initiatives take many forms. The choice for the policy-maker ranges from indirect action aimed at altering the price structure in order to encourage additional employment, through providing incentives for the public and private sectors to encourage more labour-intensive activity, to direct action establishing public sector employment-creating programmes. Such direct intervention has been attempted in over twenty countries and is being considered by many more. Rural works programmes with decentralised forms of organisation require new policies and forms of administrative organisation. In creating these, potential users of rural works may benefit from the experience of other countries. The purpose of this manual is to facilitate that process.

A Definition of Rural Works Programmes

Rural works programmes are defined as public sector activities undertaken with labour-intensive techniques with two primary objectives:

1.   generating new employment opportunities among low-income groups, and

2.   creating productive assets.

1

Introduction

There are, in addition, important subsidiary objectives such as slowing rural-urban migration and generating popular participation in national development. Such programmes are typically, but not necessarily, carried out through small-scale projects in scattered locations. Within this definition there are many variations of the basic programme concept.

This manual focuses primarily on rural rather than urban public works for two reasons. First, the public works programmes undertaken so far have been predominantly rural. To be effective in an urban environment, rural works programmes must be completely redesigned. There is little experience with such programmes specifically tailored for urban areas. Second, in quantitative terms, in most countries where total unemployment is acute, it is predominantly a rural phenomenon.

Purpose of the Manual

This manual is designed specifically for policy makers and programme administrators in those countries considering or already implementing rural works programmes as a means of alleviating unemployment. Its purpose is to organise the lessons of international experience with these programmes so that they can be applied to the policy making and implementation process of specific countries. The manual attempts to establish realistically the potentials and limitations of such programmes, to provide guidelines for deciding whether a programme can be effective in a particular area, to consider the major issues surrounding these programmes, to suggest organisational arrangements that will enhance their chances of success, and to provide criteria for judging their performance. The users of this manual will know more about their own areas and the particular environment in which they are expected to implement a rural programme than the author. While local knowledge is essential to good programme design, close examination of other rural works programmes and the compilation of experience and accumulated knowledge about this special type of development programme can be employed to benefit similar programmes in other countries.

Since rural works are a rather different form of development programme, requiring new and often highly decentralised administrative systems, and

2

because they affect political interests more tangibly than some kinds of programmes, their performance has been more varied than some other development programmes. This manual attempts to convey the lessons of experience and the guidelines which may be drawn from that experience. With this type of information, the capacity of programme administrators to alter the course and results of a programme will be greatly enhanced. The ability of the administrators to manage the programme effectively requires their viewing it as dynamic and evolving. Administrators must learn from experience as conditions change. The changes result in part from the impact of the programme.

Design of the Manual

The manual falls naturally into two major sections.

The first section deals with planning rural works programmes. Chapter Two, <u>Deciding on a Rural Works Programme</u>, provides a conceptual approach to thinking about rural works programmes. Chapter Three, <u>Evaluating the Potential of Rural Works Programmes</u>, provides criteria and suggests the data needed for judging the potential effectiveness of programmes in terms of their basic objectives. Chapter Four, <u>Major Issues in Rural Works Programmes</u>, discusses the major areas of controversy that surround these programmes and attempts to summarise the evidence that bears on the issues. The second section of the manual deals with implementation of programmes. Chapter Five, <u>Programme Organisation and Operation</u>, specifies the crucial aspects of managing a programme and the points of leverage on programme performance that the policy maker can exploit. Chapter Six, <u>Programme Monitoring</u>, provides broad performance, cost and physical standards against which the performance of a programme may be judged. The conclusion summarises the author's views as to the role and limitations of these programmes. The appendix presents a short bibliography of some of the basic books, articles, and papers on the subject.

The manual is based on wide experience with the rural works programmes of several institutions over a considerable number of years. It also draws on an international comparative study of the performance of rural works programmes. This study, funded by

Introduction

the World Bank over a two-year period, included all
the major rural works programmes at the time. In
the course of the study, visits were made to
fourteen countries, and detailed information
collected on programmes in six more countries was
included. This study culminated in a report
entitled Employment and Development: A Comparative
Analysis of the Role of Public Works Programmes. [2]
This manual is based in part on the research and
information developed in the course of that study,
supplemented by extended field experience both
before and after the study. It differs from the
earlier study in that its objective is to provide
operational guidelines and relevant information to
help officials in deciding whether a rural works
programme would be useful in a specific situation,
and in implementing such a programme.

Perspective

For nations facing acute unemployment, rural
works programmes are frequently seen as an
attractive means for attacking the interrelated
problems of unemployment, income distribution and
economic growth. However, in operation some
programmes have failed to live up to their potential
and some have proven vulnerable to misuse.

It is the view of the author of this manual
that rural works programmes are an important
instrument of development policy, but one with
limitations that must be recognised. They provide
an excellent means of alleviating unemployment and
of promoting rural development, but they are not
final solutions to these problems. They cannot
effectively reach all the unemployed. Rural works
can stimulate and augment agricultural and rural
development programmes, but they are not a
substitute for them. Therefore, the objectives of
particular programmes, the environment in which they
operated, whether they are consistent and integrated
with other policies, are some of the factors that
determine the impact they will have in a particular
area or country.

NOTES

1. The term unemployment is used to cover
both underemployment and open unemployment.

4

Introduction

2.   John W. Thomas, Shahid Javed Burki, David
G. Davies, Richard M. Hook, Employment, Etc. Report
to the World Bank, mimeo, April 1975. The World
Bank has published a summary of the report entitled
Public Works Programmes in Developing Countries: A
Comparative Analysis, World Bank Staff Working Paper
No. 224, February, 1975. Some parts of this manual
are drawn directly from the report to the Bank.

Chapter Two

DECIDING ON A RURAL WORKS PROGRAMME

A country experiencing widespread rural unemployment must consider a rural works programme as one of the available options to deal with the problem. As Chapter One suggested, rural works programmes have many common characteristics, but they are not uniform instruments. They must be designed specifically for the environment in which they will operate, and have been more successful in certain kinds of situations than others. Before thinking about programme design and organisation, administrators or planners must consider carefully whether a rural works programme can meet the objectives they have in mind, and whether the specific country conditions suggest that a programme will have a high probability of reaching these objectives.

Programme objectives are closely related to the kinds of unemployment a country is experiencing. After considering the relationship of objectives to the nature of unemployment, this chapter suggests a typology of programmes based on their dominant employment purposes. It reviews the information required to assess the need for a programme and to structure it to reach its objectives, and concludes with a review of the conditions in which rural works programmes have been effectively used.

Programme Objectives

Rural works programmes have multiple objectives, and are often seen as an attractive means for attacking the interrelated problems of unemployment, income distribution and economic growth. The primary attractions of rural works

6

programmes are as follows:

1. They have the potential to create employment without sacrificing productivity;
2. They can be implemented quickly;
3. They frequently attract foreign aid;
4. They can have a rapid and visible impact;
5. They provide benefits to a wide range of rural groups; and
6. They are very flexible as to location and timing, allowing them to be operated when and where they are needed most.

Stated major programme objectives can be ranged along a spectrum from exclusive concentration on employment creation to exclusive emphasis on asset creation. The great variation in objectives reflects the variation in underlying problems, and the fact that countries do not perceive their problems identically or order their priorities in the same way. A single country may establish several different rural works programmes in order to achieve different purposes and to reach different target groups.

In addition to employment and asset creation goals, there is another group of social and political objectives almost always present in the decision to start a rural works programme. Slowing of rural/urban migration is a frequent goal. There is often a desire to broaden participation in development efforts and to provide a vehicle for mobilising such participation. For almost any regime [1] the opportunity to undertake broad-based rural improvement has implications of creating or consolidating rural political support. Some rural works programmes have been started in an attempt to meet overtly political needs. One major national programme was initiated after the ruling party, traditionally backed by rural groups, suffered a series of unanticipated losses in by-elections. While the stated objectives for the programme were employment creation and rural assets, it was very clear that political considerations played a major role in the initiation of the programme.

A group or coalition of people within a government will support the idea of a rural works programme for rather different reasons. The different motivations must be understood by programme administrators and in some way harmonised in the programme's formulation. Political benefits are one appropriate result of a well-operated rural works programme. As discussed in a later section, a problem arises when dominating political objectives interfere with the programme's progress toward its economic and social goals.

There are great variations in objectives, national ideologies and development models, nature and severity of underlying problems and the seriousness with which governments view these problems. As a result, rural works programmes have been used as part of three distinct strategies:

1. A strategy of "tokenism in which the contribution of rural works is more cosmetic than substantive, where the size of the programme, the choice of technology and project selection and the general blend of government policies prevent the programme from having any important or lasting effect on problems of employment or equity.

2. Rural works programmes can be used to "buy time" as an interim strategy to improve welfare of target groups until slower acting but potentially stronger forces generate employment.

3. Rural works programmes can serve as reform measures where there is a real concern about rural poverty and unemployment but an inability or unwillingness to undertake thorough structural reforms, including a broad redistribution of relevant scarce resources. In such cases, substantial rural works programmes can be extremely useful in alleviating some of the effects of crisis situations, economic fluctuations, seasonal unemployment, and rural poverty. Coupled with a coherent blend of policies directed toward employment creation and some degree of income redistribution, this would appear to be the most fruitful and realistic use of this policy instrument. In such an environment, rural works programmes can serve to initiate rural organisation which may be the precursor of more comprehensive rural development programmes. They can potentially link landless labour and marginal farmers to broader rural development efforts and, if implemented in a decentralised participatory manner, bring disadvantaged rural groups together in organisational ways that may help them develop the capacity to influence policy in their own interest.

In theory, rural works programmes can usefully accompany a thorough programme of basic structural reform, including fundamental land redistribution, perhaps providing an institution for the radical organisation of peasants. Examples of rural works programmes being used in this way however appear to be very unusual.

Types of Unemployment

Unemployment and underemployment are difficult to define and measure satisfactorily in any country. The difficulties increase in most of the countries using rural works programmes because of the high proportion of employment provided by the agricultural sector and the combination of seasonal production patterns with extended family or other types of work-sharing arrangements. Nevertheless, three broad types of unemployment can be distinguished that have influenced the kinds of works programmes adopted:

1. Crisis unemployment. More than one-third of the programmes studied were introduced in response to conditions of extreme instability in agriculture caused by such recurrent crises as flood or drought.

2. Structural unemployment. The island economies of Mauritius, Jamaica and Trinidad-Tobago represent this form of unemployment, which tends to be open, long term, and frequently urban. Mauritius, as an example, is a monoculture economy with 40 per cent of total employment in the sugar industry. Sugar production is already labour intensive with no additional land available for sugar cultivation. Unemployment was estimated at 16 per cent of the labour force in 1962. Trinidad-Tobago has comparable structural problems. Overall unemployment was estimated at 15 per cent in 1972, and 26 per cent for males between 14 and 24.

3. Seasonal rural unemployment. In some of these cases, typified by Bangladesh, and parts of India and Java, agricultural land is divided into many small holdings, intensively farmed, with an increasing population sharing the work and output. The agricultural sector has a limited capacity to absorb new entrants to the rural labour force, resulting in unacceptably low income per capita and extremely high agricultural under employment in slack seasons.

A Programme Typology

The following typology classifies programmes according to their dominant employment purpose and their intended effects on target groups. In three

9

of the four categories, the classification also
reflects the nature of the underlying employment or
poverty problem.

1.   Relief Programmes. These programmes
respond to emergency conditions by supplementing or
replacing incomes reduced or destroyed by natural
calamity. They must be planned to cover at least
one full crop cycle, although provisions should be
made to permit some slowdown of activity during
planting seasons. Relief programmes are a useful
approach to emergency situations. They avoid the
psychological problems of overt relief handouts and
produce assets that may accelerate the recovery
process and diminish the prospects of subsequent
disasters. The major accent of the programme,
however, is on income distributed rather than assets
produced. Inevitably, resource constraints limit
the duration of programmes where relief is the
exclusive focus, and projects are sought which have
a higher economic payoff.

In such programmes, a backlog of simple, highly
labour-intensive projects is important because there
is little time for planning or establishing
administrative systems. Projects themselves should
be those that need the smallest inputs of materials
and technical supervision. Roads are usually the
most common projects.

2.   Long-term employment programmes. These
programmes respond to the problems of structural
unemployment. This is a necessity for long term
support of the target group since the agricultural
sector cannot absorb available labour. In theory,
long-term employment programmes should accent
training for new vocations, possible resettlement
schemes, land reclamation where possible, and give
special attention to high levels of urban
unemployment. In practice, a large part of the
target group consists of unemployed youth who are
frequently partially educated, with high employment
aspirations and a reluctance to participate in the
manual labour of conventional works programmes.
Such programmes have tended to be high cost, urban,
"make-work" efforts, with low levels of physical
productivity, sustained to deflect political dissent
among a young and potentially explosive segment of
the population. Long-term unemployment programmes
have generally been the least satisfactory form of
rural works programmes.

3.   Income augmenting programmes. This
category is the most common and the most
satisfactory in terms of meeting the dual goals of

employment and asset creation. Such programmes
supplement normal activity on the part of the target
group and, if phased properly, can obtain labour at
a relatively low opportunity cost. The target
group is generally the small freehold or tenant
farmer plus landless agricultural labour, and
workers in services or processing industries related
to agriculture. The need for seasonal
implementation suggests the importance of short-term
projects or ones that can be conveniently
interrupted during peak seasons.

4. Low cost infrastructure programmes. The
target groups for these programmes are the same as
for long-term employment or income-augmenting
programmes, but the accent is on the assets rather
than the income provided. Most of these programmes
pay very low wages. [2] Chapter Six discusses the
uses and limits of the self-help concept. In most
low-cost infrastructure programmes, as opposed to
true self-help projects, the target groups do not
receive the benefits from the assets created. In
such cases, low-cost infrastructure programmes
paying sub-standard wages represent a regressive
form of taxation and should not be undertaken.

These distinctions between types of programmes
are not permanent; programmes can and do start off
with one predominant set of objectives and move to
another over time. For example, many programmes
start as relief, as did Morocco and Tunisia, but in
time shift to the income-augmenting category.

Planners should be aware that a national rural
works programme, once started, will probably become
permanent. No country which started this activity
in the 1960s has ended it. Programme titles and
purposes change, but the basic involvement continues
as rural expectations are aroused, bureaucratic
procedures and staff are established and interest
groups recognise the value of the programme to
themselves.

Assessing the Need for a Rural Works Programme

In order to assess the need for a rural works
programme and to help determine the type of
programme that is needed, administrators require
detailed micro information on a number of questions:

1. Data on the extent, location, and
seasonality of under- and unemployment are required
to plan the size, timing and location of the
programme.

2. Information on the economic and social characteristics of target groups. The reasons for their unemployment, the pattern of their non-agricultural activities and employment, and other factors affecting their ability and desire to accept rural works employment must be known. Designations such as "the unemployed" or "the rural poor" are inadequate for rural works planning. The more accurately target groups can be specified, the greater the chance of establishing a programme that will in fact reach them.

3. Information on the existence, location and condition of rural infrastructure assets, and the potential for developing them using primarily unskilled labour is required to determine whether there is scope for rural works and to predict programme economic returns.

4. Information on administrative and technical competence, public and private, at local and intermediate levels is essential for the administrative design.

5. Data on the nature of income and asset distribution (particularly land) in areas where rural works are planned is needed to predict the distribution of benefits.

6. Information on density of population, incidence of unemployment on a disaggregated basis and labour supply response at given wage rates is necessary to determine whether sufficient numbers of workers will be available.

Situations Where Rural Works Have Been Effective

Rural works programmes can be useful instruments in many, but not all, developing countries which experience problems of rural unemployment and poverty. It may be helpful to the planner who is considering such a programme to look at the common characteristics of countries that have used works programmes successfully. There is no clear-cut "rural works" profile, but a number of generalisations can be made.

1. High Population Density. The clearest characteristic of countries using these programmes on a national basis is their high population density in relation to cultivable land and a resulting heavy pressure on agricultural resources. Pressure on cultivable land is particularly prevalent in the countries of South and South East Asia which have used these programmes effectively: Indonesia, for

Table 2.1.—Classification of Programmes

Employment Creation <--> Asset Creation

Relief	Income Augmentation	Low-cost Infrastructure

Afghanistan
  Provincial Development
	Bangladesh
	  The Works Programme
		Columbia
		  Pico y Pala

Brazil
  Departamento Nacional
  de Obras Contra as Sêcas
	India
	  Crash Scheme for Rural
	  Employment
	  Drought Prone Areas Programme
		Indonesia
		  DESA
		  Padat Karya

India
  Scarcity Relief
	Indonesia
	  Kabupaten
		Ethiopia
		  Tigre Development
		  Organisation

	South Korea Self Help Work Programme	
Long-term Employment	Morocco Promotion Nationale	

Jamaica
  Special Employment Programmes
	Pakistan
	  Rural Works Programme	

Mauritius
  Relief Workers Programme
  Travail Pour Tous
  Rural Development Project
	Tunisia
	  Lutte Contre le Sous
	  Developpement (LCSD)	

Trinidad-Tobago
  Special Works Programme
  Prime Minister's Special
  Works Programme		

13

example, with a population of about 600 per cultivated square kilometre, or Bangladesh and the Republic of Korea with over 1,000 people per cultivated square kilometre. With the exception of Tunisia and Morocco, countries with national programmes are all among the most crowded one-third of the developing nations, and these two exceptions share with the others high ratios of population to cultivable land.

High densities in relation to resources often result in fractionated land holdings and spreading available work among members of an increasing labour force with low levels of average income and productivity. Coupled with seasonal agricultural patterns, these conditions assure a need for seasonal income supplements and a large potential labour force. The latter is very important if a rural works programme is to follow the typical pattern, a large number of small projects with workers recruited from local residents. For example, assume that a small project requires a work force of forty people, and workers are willing to go as far as five kilometres to get to the work site. If the labour force participation rate is 35 per cent, and the programme can reach 2 per cent of the labour force (both are typical figures), the required population density is over fifty people per square kilometre.

In sparsely populated areas, typical of much of Africa and the mid-East, population densities are too low to implement programmes of this sort. In such areas, it would be necessary to transport workers to and from projects or to provide them with housing, food and other amenities at the work sites. This can be done, but it is more costly, requires a high level of organisation and supporting inputs, and is more disruptive of existing employment and social patterns. If a country has sharply differing regional patterns of population density and pressure, it may be preferable to limit the programme to the more populous areas or to set up two types of programmes--the traditional small projects in the regions of dense population, and larger centralised projects with workers brought to, or kept at, the work site in the less populous areas. Experience with the latter approach in Tunisia suggests that workers tend to form a permanent rural works force, moving from site to site. While this provides employment, it defeats the common purpose of organising a programme that supplements rather than supplants existing patterns.

14

2. Agricultural Dependence and Instability.
National public works programmes are typically used
by countries with high dependence on agriculture in
terms of proportion of labour force and contribution
to G.D.P. These programmes work best in
agricultural settings. As discussed in Chapter Four,
public works programmes have been generally
ineffective in urban areas.

There is a strong positive correlation between
instability of agricultural output (particularly
food crops) and the use of rural works programmes.
This is not surprising since many programmes
originate in conditions of crisis, following crop
failure or threat of famine. In North Africa, for
example, the programmes in Tunisia and Morocco arose
in the context of fragile economies where year-to-
year declines of 30 per cent or more in cereal grain
output have been experienced.

3. Per Capita Income. The countries that have
used rural works programmes are poor, but measured
on a per capita income basis they are not the
poorest of the developing countries. Of the thirty
poorest countries, only two, Bangladesh and
Afghanistan, have national programmes. This
reflects the interaction of several factors. Many
of the poorest countries, the majority of which are
in sub-Saharan Africa, have very small populations
relative to agricultural area. They often have a
large shifting or nomadic population, making it
difficult to implement the typical rural works
project.

A related factor is administrative competence.
Setting up a large number of work sites across a
country requires a basic bureaucratic and
administrative competence at local levels. Most
countries with effective rural works programmes have
inherited or built up such competence. Where it is
lacking--Afghanistan's experience with its
Provincial Development Programme in 1971-72 is a
good example--programmes have suffered from poor
administration and low quality projects.

A country considering such a programme should
make sure it has the needed capabilities, at a level
at least as decentralised as the district in South
Asia or the governorate in North Africa, for
planning, implementation and control. If not, rural
works programmes should be introduced only in those
areas where such capacity exists, and deferred
elsewhere until staff and institutional structures
can be developed to identify local needs, organise
work forces, arrange for the timely delivery of

inputs, and ensure execution in accordance with reasonable technical standards. [3]

The composite picture of a country or a region that is a likely candidate for a successful rural works programme looks like this: a high dependence on agriculture, heavy population pressures on agricultural resources, settled population patterns, a record of instability in production of food crops, and an administrative capacity sufficiently developed to provide the needed decentralised skills.

NOTES

1.   The term regime is used here without intending the negative implications which usually accompany it, but rather to identify the top leadership within a government, both political and bureaucratic that makes basic policy decisions.

2.   Pico y Pala in Columbia is an interesting exception. It is a low-cost infrastructure programme that pays premium wages in a road-building programme in mountainous parts of the country.

3. The issue of speed versus capability is discussed in more detail in Chapter Four.

Chapter Three

EVALUATING THE POTENTIAL OF RURAL WORKS PROGRAMMES

Once a planner or administrator has decided
that conditions favour the adoption of a rural works
programme, what realistic expectations can he have
as to the programme's potential contribution? This
chapter will discuss the extent to which a rural
works programme can be expected to provide benefits
in the areas of employment, asset creation and
distribution. As a starting point, it is useful to
introduce two sets of distinctions that will be used
in much of the discussion that follows: first,
between the construction and the operation of
projects, and, second, between categories of
projects.

Construction and Operating Phases

During the construction phase, the principal
benefit is the direct employment provided to the
people working on the project. During the operating
phase, the principal beneficiaries are the reci-
pients of the services flowing from the completed
assets, plus the workers employed in the operation
and maintenance of the projects.

Categories of Projects

The type of project that is selected is also an
important determinant of the contribution a rural
works programme can make to employment, growth and
equity goals. It is helpful to divide projects into
the following three groups:

1. Directly Productive Projects. These are
    projects which lead directly to increased

production, generally in agriculture.
Irrigation, drainage which allows
additional crops to be grown, and land
reclamation, are examples of directly
productive projects.
2. Economic Infrastructure. These are
projects which do not directly produce
additional output, but which provide
necessary supporting infrastructure to
promote output and growth indirectly. The
most common of such projects is road
construction. Conservation projects and
market development also fall into this
category.
3. Social Infrastructure. Schools or health
clinics or community buildings are the type
of social facilities easily developed
through rural works.

Most rural works programmes have included
projects in all three categories, but economic
infrastructure assets have clearly dominated, as
shown in Table 3.1. This dominance reflects the
high priority given in many programmes to the
construction and repair of secondary and feeder
roads. While accurate figures are not available in
all cases, such projects probably account for at
least 50 per cent of total rural works activity.

The Employment Goal

Employment creation is one of several goals of
rural works which are pursued simultaneously. [1] A
planner needs to know how to estimate realistically
the employment contribution that a well-operated
programme can make, both in the construction and in
the operating phase. Unemployment can take many
forms, ranging from permanently unemployed urban
workers to rural landless labourers who may find
paid employment in only four or five months of the
year. There are the educated unemployed, the
seasonally underemployed, and informal sector
workers putting in long hours every day at extremely
low levels of income. Rural works programmes can
deal quite effectively with some of these groups but
are unable to have significant impact on others.
The planner needs detailed information on the size,
location and nature of the unemployment problem,
including information on the characteristics of the
un- and underemployed groups.

Table 3.1.--Profile of Rural Works Project Expenditures

Country	Directly productive [a]	Economic infra- structure[b]	Social infra- structure[c]
	(per cent of total expenditure)		
Afghanistan (1971-72)	12	82	6
Bangladesh (1963-72)	7.2	76.6	16.2
Brazil (1909-59) [d]	50	50	0
Columbia (1972-77)	0	100	0
Ethiopia (1971-72) (Tigre Province)	15.7	84.3	0
India (Drought Prone Area) (1970-77)	47.4	50.5	2.2
(Crash Scheme) (1971-77)	14	77	9
Indonesia (Kubupaten) (1970-77)	14.3	71.2	14.5
Mauritius (1971-77)	25.4	41.3	33.2
Morocco (1961-77)	30.2	50.7	19.1
Pakistan (1961-72)	23.2	30.5	46.4
Peru (CORPUNO) (1962-65)	27	35	43
South Korea NCS (1961-63)	46	48	6
Self Help Work (1964-72)	58.3	32.5	9.2
Tunisia (1958-77)	23.9	44.5	30.7
Unweighted average	26.2	58.1	15.7

a. Includes irrigation, drainage, land reclamation and bench terracing projects and fisheries and development of veterinary centres.

b. Includes construction of roads, culverts and bridges, flood control, market development, rural electrification, land conservation and reafforestation .

c. Includes construction of schools, clinics, community buildings, low-cost housing and parks and drinking water systems.

d. Estimate.

19

1. <u>Construction Phase Employment.</u> In the construction phase, a rural works programme is most
effective in reaching the rural, seasonally unemployed who are already members of the agricultural
labour force. The groups most frequently employed
are landless labourers, small tenant farmers and
small proprietor farmers whose holdings are insufficient to provide adequate levels of employment and
income. There are other groups that can be quite
difficult to reach directly through such programmes.
These groups include the very young, the very old,
the ill, the malnourished, and frequently, women.
Rural works employment is usually physically
demanding, thus eliminating persons incapable of
hard physical labour. If an employment criterion is
used, there are large numbers of underemployed
people whose time is fully occupied in agricultural
or service activities and who are therefore not
available. In some countries, traditional employment arrangements for landless labourers bind them
to a patron on an annual basis. Such labourers may
not be permitted to take rural works employment even
if their patron does not need them. If they are
employed, they may be required to give their
earnings to their patron. In some countries, caste
or other social distinctions make it impossible for
certain unemployed persons to accept rural works
employment. Potential employees for rural works
programmes must possess four qualifications: (1)
they must be poor enough to need and want supplemen-
tal income, (2) they must be available in the sense
of having time free for construction phase employment, (3) they must be willing to accept this type
of employment, and (4) they must be physically
capable of doing the work. Those not having these
characteristics will not benefit from construction
phase employment.

With these limitations in mind, how effective
can a works programme be in reducing unemployment?
Table 3.2 shows the number of days of work per
member of the labour force represented by total
construction phase employment in a number of rural
works programmes. Working from these figures, and
using official estimates of unemployment, the
largest programme, Tunisia's, absorbed about 20 per
cent of total unemployment, during the 1960s. In
Morocco, a similar approach suggests that the
programme there absorbed about 14 per cent of
estimated unemployment in the 1960s. Major
programmes in other countries had smaller, though
still substantial, impact: about 7 per cent of

Evaluating the Potential of Rural Works Programmes

Table 3.2.--Relative Significance and Cost of Rural Works in Creating Employment

Country	Programme	Period	Annual average worker-days of employment generated by public works (in millions)	Annual average worker-days generated per member of labour force (in days)	Direct cost per worker-day of employment created (US$)
Afghanistan	Provincial Development	1971-72	4.7	1.3	0.98
Bangladesh	Works Programme	1962-77	28.8	1.5	0.97
Columbia	Pico y Pala	1972-77	1.0	*	3.87
Ethiopia	Tigre Development Organisation	1971-74	0.3	0.2	0.32
India	Crash Scheme for Rural Employment	1971-77	178.0	1.0	0.50
	Drought Prone Areas Programme	1970-77	37.9	0.2	0.67
Indonesia	Kabupaten Programme	1970-77	37.0	0.9	0.71
Jamaica	Special Employment Programme	1974	2.5	3.5	9.15
Mauritius	Travail Pour Tous	1971-74	1.4	5.5	1.85
Morocco	Promotion Nationale	1961-77	15.9	3.1	0.88
Pakistan	Rural Works	1963-72	4.4	0.3	3.17
South Korea	Self Help Work Programme	1964-72	29.1	2.9	0.57
Trinidad-Tobago	Special Works Programme	1965-77	0.5	1.3	7.80
Tunisia	LCSD	1958-77	28.8	20.7	0.75

* Not available.

21

total unemployment for Korea in the late 1960s, and 3.4 per cent of agricultural unemployment in East Pakistan in 1968. On balance, it appears that a well-financed and effectively administered programme might realistically succeed in absorbing as much as 10 per cent of estimated unemployment. To go far beyond that figure would frequently strain the budgetary and administrative resources that are available, and would encounter the limits of available workers. [2]

The type of assets built under a rural works programme will also influence the amount of construction phase labour that is created. While technologies and labour intensities vary between programmes and within programmes (building roads in rocky versus soft terrains, for example), some generalisations can be made. Economic infrastructure assets are often the most effective creators of construction phase employment. Such activities as flood protection, water conservation and soil conservation can be carried out with minimal use of materials and highly skilled labour. Secondary and feeder roads, the greatest single type of rural works expenditures, can also use highly labour-intensive techniques. To the extent that bridges and culverts are required, the proportion of unskilled labour used, will, of course, decline.

Directly productive projects generally create less employment in the construction phase. Material costs for many of these projects, such as cement and pipes for minor irrigation works, are higher than in projects which involve earthmoving alone. In addition, more skilled labour is frequently required in relation to total labour costs. Since social infrastructure projects generally involve the construction of buildings, they have the highest skilled labour and materials components of the three categories.

2. Operating Phase Employment. Employment creation during the operating phase of projects is difficult to predict since it depends on a number of variables including the mix of projects, their productivity, the degree of coordination with other development activities, etc. However, a number of useful generalisations can be made.

It is important to recognise that there are substantial long-term employment benefits in the operating phase which must receive attention. In none of the rural works programmes studied was there any specific forecast of long-range employment creation suggesting that important opportunities for

<u>long-term employment creation have been lost.</u>
The type of project with the greatest potential
for employment generation is the repair and
restoration of obsolescent directly productive
assets, such as irrigation and drainage systems. In
some cases, one worker-day in the construction phase
has resulted in more than two days of annual
employment during the operating phase (see Table
3.3). Since such projects also have high economic
returns, in terms of increased production, they
should be sought out and given a very high priority.
Directly productive projects creating new assets
also have a high operating phase employment payoff.
As shown in Table 3.3, irrigation and land reclamation projects in the Republic of Korea and in
India have produced one worker-day of agricultural
employment for each 2.5 to 5.2 worker-days during
the construction phase. If the life of these
projects is estimated conservatively at five years,
one worker-day of construction phase employment
creates more than one worker-day of agricultural
employment over the life of the project. These
calculations understate the total number of
employment opportunities resulting from the
operating phase of projects since they ignore the
implications of expansion in non-agricultural
activities associated with the increased agricultural output.

Economic infrastructure projects also create
jobs in the operating phase, but in ways that are
difficult to quantify. Roads mean more vehicles,
and with them, construction, operation and maintenance requirements. They enlarge markets and
promote a monetised economy which inevitably means
more employment. Social infrastructure assets have
the lowest operating phase employment potential of
the three types of projects, creating little direct
employment other than the need for skilled teachers
or medical personnel. In the long run, improved
education and health facilities may increase productivity or employability of workers, but the impact
is so difficult to measure that it cannot be easily
included in the benefits of rural works.

<u>Overall, a rural works programme with a
balanced profile of projects should be capable of
producing long-term employment in a proportion of
one long-term job opportunity for each five or six
worker-years of construction phase employment.</u>
Creation of long-term employment is an important
potential contribution and should be considered when
eligible types of projects are selected.

Table 3.3--Long-term Employment Creation from Rural Works Irrigation and
Drainage Projects

Country	Area Benefited	Cost	Total construction employment in worker-days	Long-term agricultural employment created [a]	Employment ratio [b]
	(000ha)	(000 US$)	(000)	(000)	
Reconstruction					
Bangladesh (drainage)[c]	34.3d	532	723	1,526	1/2.1
Indonesia (irrigation)[e]	106.9	3,078	4,348	9,240	1/2.2
New construction					
South Korea Irrigation					
(1961-63)[f]	75.7	39,500	19,000	6,545	2.5/1g
(1964-68)[h]	13.6	2,442	4,522	1,173	4.1/1g
Land reclamation	14.5	2,968	5,498	1,248	4.3/1
Tidelands terracing	12.2	2,936	5,437	1,054	5.2/1
India (irrigation)[i] Mysore State	0.2	62	93	21	4.5/1

a In worker days per year.
b The ratio of construction-worker-days to permanent-worker-days.
c Government of East Pakistan, Performance Report: Works Programme 1967-68.
d Area benefited is reduced by a factor of 2.3 since Thomas (1971) found that irrigation benefits are generally overestimated by a factor of 2.3.
e W. P. Falcon, Belinda Dapise and Richard Patten, "An Experiment in Rural Employment Creation: Indonesia's Kabupaten Program," mimeo. (1973).
f Daniel Kie-Hong Lee, "National Construction Services: Korea's Experiences in Utilization of Underdeveloped Manpower Resources," mimeo. (1969).
g Evidence from the sources cited for this table suggests that the labour input for one crop of irrigated rice in Indonesia, Bangladesh and India ranges from 148 to 247 days per hectare. On the basis of this, 185 days per crop per hectare was taken as the average. Irrigation was assumed to produce 86 worker-days additional labour per hectare and drainage 44 worker-days.
h Republic of Korea, Ministry of Health and Social Affairs, "Self Help Work Program," (1968).
i Graeme Donovan, "Rural Works and Employment: Description and Preliminary Analysis of a Land Army Project in Mysore State, India," Occasional Paper No. 60, Employment and Income Distribution Project, Cornell University.

Asset Creation and Development Goals

Most countries cannot undertake rural works projects strictly as transfer payment mechanisms; they must also contribute to development through the creation of useful assets. Therefore, it is essential to analyze the degree to which rural works contribute to the goal of growth and development. For a rural works programme to be successful in meeting its mixed economic objectives, there must be scope for labour-intensive construction projects that can be carried out at acceptable rates of return. If there are very limited opportunities for such projects, there is little hope of a sustained works programme.

1. Existing Economic Analyses. Table 3.4 shows the results of analyses of rural works projects in five countries: Bangladesh, Ethiopia, Indonesia, Mauritius and Morocco. In these five, benefit-cost ratios or internal rates of return were calculated and the results indicate quite reasonable returns in purely economic terms.

The Morocco study is particularly interesting. [3] One of the authors calculated returns on ten Promotion Nationale projects in three categories: small- and medium-scale irrigation, and soil conservation. Wages were not shadow priced. Small-scale irrigation projects, constructing distribution systems for existing water sources, show an internal rate of return of 24.4 per cent; medium-scale irrigation projects, building water control structures to harness flood waters, show a rate of 12.9 per cent; and soil conservation projects show a rate of 6.0 per cent. The study also compares rates of return on eight Promotion Nationale projects with 11 generally similar projects carried out by other governmental departments, without the specific use of the Promotion Nationale labour-intensive approach. The Promotion Nationale projects showed an average internal rate of return significantly higher than the departmental projects.

The number of cost-benefit studies of rural works programmes is limited. However, the studies that exist show that rural works can be productive in rigorous economic terms; if they become inefficient make-work programmes, it is a result of poor planning and implementation.

It should be noted that cost-benefit analysis cannot capture all the benefits of some types of projects. Those focused on social infrastructure creation cannot be adequately assessed using this

Table 3.4.--Benefit-cost Analysis of Rural Works Programmes

Country	Types of projects	Internal rate of return (per cent)	Benefit-cost ratio	Was labour shadow-priced?	Comment
Bangladesh	Roads, drainage flood control	--	3.4	No	Benefit-cost ratio for total programme at 12% discount rate
Ethiopia	Terracing and reafforestation	18.4	--	Yes	
	Irrigation	--	2.0	No	12% discount rate
Indonesia	Roads	--	3.6	No	Discounted, but rate unknown
Mauritius	Land improvement	13.8	--	No	
	Irrigation	14.3	--	Yes	
Morocco	Irrigation	18.2	--	No	
	Conservation	6.0	--	--	

NOTE: The use of (--) indicates not available.

technique, since the benefits cannot be as easily quantified as with directly productive projects. Returns on economic infrastructure projects are difficult to quantify in detail, but if the projects are carried out with relative efficiency they should yield acceptable returns. Feeder or farm-to-market roads can make important contributions to increased production and the development of agriculture-related services and small-scale industries.

Conservation and reafforestation projects and flood embankments may not produce immediate income for people, but tend to promote increased economic activity and returns over a longer period of time, and do more to prevent future losses than to provide immediate benefits. This may be just as important a function as creating assets with new benefit flows, and the long-term benefits may conceivably exceed those of either roads or directly productive projects.

2. Availability of Productive Projects. Not all projects can be carried out appropriately by means of a labour-intensive rural works programme. Depending on the existing state of rural infra-structure and the opportunities for directly productive projects which can be performed with a labour-intensive technology, there may or may not be an adequate supply of potentially attractive projects. Therefore, the programme planner must know in some detail the nature and adequacy of the existing infrastructure, and the need for projects which can be undertaken efficiently by labour-intensive means.

The productivity of projects is also influenced greatly by the general objectives of the programme. Projects that are primarily relief-oriented and which stress employment creation will frequently produce lower returns than projects which aim at income augmentation within a larger development strategy. If opportunities for labour-intensive projects exist in large supply, one of the preconditions of a rural works programme is satisfied. However, the potential for such projects must also be viewed from the perspective of population, location, and stage of agricultural development. Economic returns to rural works programmes will be higher in areas where agriculture is growing rapidly. It is obvious that where agriculture is productive, new technologies used, and economic activity brisk, facilities such as roads, drainage or irrigation will have high returns. However, a country may want to use a public works programme in the opposite way, as a stimulus to regions that are not growing. Economic infrastructure, particularly, can be of great importance in generating new activity in backward regions. Thus, a rural works programme can be used for regional development in an area that is poorer than the rest of the country. It is therefore necessary for the programme planner to view returns and project selection in the perspective of other development considerations.

Distributive Effects

Rural works programmes are increasingly seen as possible vehicles for raising income levels of the poor, and perhaps redistributing assets toward the economically disadvantaged portions of the population. By themselves, these programmes are generally not capable of any major redistribution, but can have moderately redistributive effects. Planners and administrators should be aware of the variables that determine the distributive impact of a programme in order to increase the probability of achieving its distributional goals.

1. Importance of Labour Payments. Employment of labour in the construction phase of projects is the most directly income-augmenting aspect of rural works programmes, particularly in respect to unskilled labour. Table 3.5 shows the proportion of programme costs represented by wage payments for 16 programmes in 14 countries. In some cases we have adjusted the reported percentage downward where we believe that official programme reports overstated labour payments, or ignored substantial amounts of non-labour expenses. Labour intensity will differ by project type, wage scale and technology, which accounts for the extremely wide range of figures reported.

It must be concluded that even the most labour-intensive famine relief programmes cannot be expected to surpass labour intensities reflected by allocations of 75 per cent of programme costs to wages. Income augmenting programmes producing assets of acceptable quality should be spending 55 per cent to 65 per cent of programme funds on wages. If less than 50 per cent of programme expenditures are devoted to wage payments, important questions are raised as to the seriousness of the employment creation goal and the appropriateness of the technology and/or wage scale that is being used.

2. Wage Rates. Wage rates, along with the use of labour-intensive techniques, determine the extent of benefits to the poor in the construction phase of projects. Many programmes reflect the view that self-help contributions from the local community which obtains the benefits should be part of the programme. As a form of recapturing some of the cost of the programmes, by taxing the benefits, this is perfectly legitimate. However, it is only in a minority of the cases that the programme's target groups, unemployed, generally unskilled labour, receive a substantial share of the benefits from projects. Therefore, the wage mechanism is crucial to the programme's objective of assisting low-income groups. The use of wages at substantially less than market rates is in effect a tax on low-income groups and should be avoided.

3. The Operating Phase. In the operating phase, it is much more difficult to ensure that benefits reach target groups than it is in the construction phase. The division of benefits will tend to follow the division of relevant scarce resources, particularly land. Directly productive projects, such as minor irrigation works, which allow an additional crop, will create additional job opportunities, provided production is carried out in a labour-intensive fashion. However, the returns to landowners will be larger than the benefits to workers through additional employment. In a typical irrigation project allowing an additional crop of rice to be cultivated in a labour-intensive fashion, it was calculated that the additional benefits flowing to landowners and benefits accruing to labour were in a ratio of 3.5 to 1.0. [4] The benefits to labour can still be important, however. In the irrigation scheme just mentioned, up to 250 worker days of additional labour per hectare were created.

If a programme can be designed so that the assets created benefit low-income groups directly, the impact on rural poverty will be greatly enhanced. If productive assets are created (terraces or reclamation) and the assets can be distributed to low-income groups, their income potential will be greatly increased. In addition, if projects can be carried out in areas inhabited primarily by low-income groups, it is clear that their share of the benefits will increase.

Similarly, economic infrastructure projects will direct most of their benefits to landowners where the project is located. But benefits, while

Table 3.5.—Wage Payment as a Percentage of Total Rural Works Expenditure

Country	Programme	Percentage	Notes
High employment creation (60% or over for wages)			
Columbia	Pico y Pala	66	
Bangladesh	Works Programme (1962-67)	63	Refers to pre-separation period to 1971. No data available from 1967-71.
India	Crash Scheme for Rural Employment	76	
South Korea	National Construction Service	69	
	Self-help Work Programme	70-75	The official figure of 85% is suspect. Field interviews suggest local contributions of land and labour are not included in official totals. The addition of local contributions suggests the lower amount shown here.
Medium employment creation (40% to 60% for wages)			
Afghanistan	Provincial Development	55	Calculated from 1973-74 estimates of programme resource requirements.
India	Drought Prone Areas Programme	50	Official estimate.
Mauritius	Travail Four Tous	53	
Morocco	Promotion Nationale	50	Official figure of 83% highly suspect. Substantial local and intermediate-level contributions are not included in total cost. This estimate based on observations and comparisons with other programmes.

Table 3.5, continued

Country	Programme	Percentage	Notes
Trinidad-Tobago	Prime Minister's Special Works Programme	51	Estimates on the basis of total wage payments.
Tunisia	Lutte Contre le Sous Developpement	50	Official reports state that 90% of programme expenditures go to wages. These exclude contributions at the Governate level. Data on three projects in different Governates show the labour component of expenditures to be 51%, 36% and 61%.
Low employment creation (less than 40% for wages)			
Bangladesh	The Works Programme (excluding Test Relief)	16	From a 1973 survey.
Brazil	Northeast Drought Relief	25	
Ethiopia	Tigre Province, Food for Work	25	Estimate.
Indonesia	IMPRES or Kabupaten Programme	28	The materials used in this programme are also labour-intensive. If the wage component of the cost of materials were included, wages would represent some 60% of total programme expenditures.
Pakistan	Rural Works Programme	]	Figures incorporate all costs, including land, which is generally not included in other countries' costs.
	People's Works Programme	] 35	

31

difficult to quantify, will not be limited to land holders. Feeder road systems or enlarged markets inevitably mean more jobs. In theory, the distribution of benefits from social infrastructure projects is quite wide. A new school or clinic can benefit an entire community. However, one cannot always assume this wide distribution and in some cases action must be taken to ensure that it will occur. Discrimination against low-income groups may take many forms, intentional as well as unintentional. Cost is the most obvious. School fees or clinic charges may exceed what some individuals are able to pay. Among the poorest groups, children have to work in the fields or assist at home during peak labour seasons and may drop out of of school during this period. Special supporting services may be required if the full distributive potential of social infrastructure projects is to be realised.

Table 3.6 compares the three categories of projects in terms of economic returns, social returns, redistribution effects and employment creation.

4. Sharing Benefits with Non-Target Groups. Almost inevitably some programme benefits will go to non-target groups. Within limits, this can be an advantage. The provision of rural assets that stimulate development across a broad range of the rural populace is obviously desirable. Most rural works programmes are decentralised in administration and need the capacity of local officials and sometimes the active cooperation of local craftsmen, contractors, etc. This mobilising of local talent is much easier to achieve if a broad base of the population is benefiting in some degree from programme activities. In addition, benefits to non-target groups help develop political support for a programme that has some redistributive content and is otherwise likely to encounter strong political opposition. Carefully managed, this breadth of distribution of benefits can be an advantage.

Table 3.6.--Performance of Different Types of Projects in Meeting Programme Objectives

Type of project	Economic returns	Social returns	Redistributive effects	Employment created
Directly productive (irrigation, land reclamation, drainage, etc.)	High	Low	Highly variable (depends on who owns land improved)	In construction--medium. In operation--high.
Economic infrastructure (roads, conservation, flood control, markets, afforestation)	Medium	Medium	Medium	In construction--high. In operation--medium.
Social infrastructure (schools, clinics, community buildings)	Low	High	High (if low-income groups have access to facilities)	In construction--low. In operation--low.

NOTES

1.   The issue of conflicts and tradeoffs between goals is examined in Chapter 4.

2.   Full recognition must be given, however, to the income effect of this employment. In East Pakistan, it was calculated that rural works employment provides a 75 per cent to 100 per cent increase in annual income for large numbers of underemployed small farmers.

3. Rajaona Andriamananjara, "Labour Mobilization: The Moroccan Experience," CRED Occasional Paper 15, University of Michigan, Ann Arbor, 1971.

4.   See Thomas et al. Employment and Development p. 119 for the calculation of this figure.

Chapter Four

MAJOR ISSUES IN RURAL WORKS PROGRAMMES

There are a number of basic issues which
surround rural works programmes, and which influence
the decision as to whether such a programme should
be adopted. It is important for planners and
administrators to be aware of these issues in
shaping the decisions to proceed and in anticipating
questions and criticisms that will be directed
toward existing programmes. Rural works programmes
have given rise to extensive controversy, with
exaggerated claims made on both the positive and
negative side. They have been attacked as wasteful
and inefficient. On the other hand, excessive
claims have been made as to their potential for
eliminating unemployment and developing the rural
areas. The purpose of this chapter is to raise
several fundamental issues, summarise the arguments
and evidence on both sides and provide a balanced
view as to how the issue should influence the
decision to undertake a programme, and how it might
shape its priorities, size, design and operation.

Economic Efficiency

How efficient are labour-intensive rural works
projects in benefit-cost terms? In Chapter Three, a
number of studies of these programmes were reviewed
briefly. The conclusion was reached that a well
planned and implemented rural works programme with a
variety of projects in all three categories of
directly productive, economic infrastructure and
social infrastructure, should show benefit-cost
ratios and internal rates of return that are
comparable to those expected from good projects in
other types of development programmes. The question
is sometimes restated to ask whether labour-

intensive projects show higher returns than projects using other technologies. This approach fails to emphasise the employment and distributive aims of rural works programmes. If the question is to be asked in that form, it is also appropriate to develop a framework for evaluation that assigns distributive weights to benefits going to different groups of beneficiaries. There is a considerable volume of recently completed and continuing research regarding the optimal mix (in terms of lowest cost combination of inputs for a given output) of labour and capital in the construction of facilities, particularly roads, in rural areas. While the evidence available so far does not permit firm conclusions as to the relative efficiency of labour- intensive techniques, it does suggest that labour-intensive techniques can be efficient. [1]

In four of the six benefit-cost studies referred to in Chapter Two, shadow wage rates were not used. In countries where unemployment is extremely high, it is likely that shadow pricing on the basis of social opportunity cost would result in higher rates of return. The Bangladesh and Morocco studies were carried out ex post and showed lower returns than the four ex ante studies. This difference suggests that the failure of individual projects and programmes to achieve their economic aims is a result of implementational failures rather than an inherent weakness in the application of labour-intensive technology to small rural projects. Important factors contributing to the ability of projects to reach their potential include the following:

1. Planning and Technical Adequacy. The best protection against failures in this area is to insist on a limited list of eligible projects, using standard specifications, and simplified operating manuals, and to establish specific project preparation techniques as suggested in Chapter 4.

2. Labour Efficiency. Adequate wage scales, comparable to seasonal minimum agricultural wages, incentive systems based on standardised work norms, and supervisory techniques which take into account traditional forms of labour organisation can help raise standards of labour efficiency. In many countries, for example, workers will arrive at the work site in groups based on village, family or clan relationships. Such work groups frequently include a mutually acceptable leader who can assign tasks within the group, promote efficient time use and supplement scarce supervisory talent.

Individual instances of gross inefficiency were encountered in most programmes. This is not a problem which is unique to rural works programmes, although it is accentuated by the stretching of supervisory staff to cover large numbers of small dispersed projects. The steps suggested above will help eliminate the stereotyped image of rural works employees being paid to lean on their shovels or sit in the shade.

3. Seasonal Employment Patterns and Opportunity Costs. Seasonal patterns of demand for agricultural labour vary widely between different areas. For example, in the rice growing areas of Bangladesh, where irrigation permits three crops per year, the rural labour force approaches full employment for about 135 days. In the irrigated areas of Pakistan, where two crops are possible in a year, periods of full employment total about 110 days. [2] If rural works activities are not planned to take account of such local variations the opportunity cost of labour may rise sharply.

In general, most programmes did an effective job of coordinating rural works activity with seasonal needs, concluding, deferring or inter-rupting projects in order to avoid conflicts during periods of peak seasonal employment. There were individual instances of poor coordination in almost all programmes. Farmers in Tunisia, Morocco and Trinidad-Tobago have complained about the diminution of agricultural labour supply as a result of rural works programmes, and in the Padat Karya programme in Indonesia, workers themselves have suggested a better phasing of projects so as to avoid competi-tion with their primary income earning activities in agriculture. [3] In Morocco it was reported that insufficient labour was available for certain rural works projects which were not phased to take account of agricultural seasonality.

Long-term employment programmes offering year-round jobs can present problems of seasonal adjust-ment if they are combined with high wage scales. In Trinidad-Tobago, for example, it was decided to pay all programme employees the government minimum wage of US $4.00 per day which, based on urban industrial wages, was almost twice the agricultural wage rate. In this case, because the works programme was not seasonal, it was able to outbid the agricultural sector for labour in peak seasons and resulted in a labour shortage in agriculture.

These examples point up the necessity for a close analysis of seasonality and alternative

employment opportunities in order to avoid undesirable increases in opportunity costs. From the
programme planner's and administrator's view, they
suggest the importance of short or interruptible
projects, the necessity for adherence to a well
defined annual schedule of project approvals, funds
allocations, coordination with worksite delivery of
complementary inputs, and the potential risks
involved in using contractors who may be unable or
unwilling to accommodate their operation to seasonal
agricultural patterns.

    4. <u>Project Choice</u>. As suggested in Chapter
Three, directly productive projects and infrastructure projects, both economic and social, can
all yield good economic returns. Make-work projects
such as leaf-raking and pavement-sweeping should be
avoided. Such wasteful projects have been reported
in a number of programmes, including the early
efforts in Mauritius, and the Special Employment
Programme in Jamaica (referred to at times as the
"Christmas Programme" because of employing people in
non-productive jobs to provide income for the
holiday season).

    While acceptable benefit-cost performance must
be expected in any continuing rural works programme,
there is a danger that excessive concern with
economic performance can impede the successful
functioning of a programme. When feasibility
studies are done preparatory to starting a
programme, benefit-cost analyses of typical project
types are essential. Similarly, periodic evalua-
tions of programme effectiveness are desirable,
including an effort to analyse on an <u>ex-post</u> basis,
the extent to which anticipated benefits have been
achieved. On a day-to-day basis, however, these
programmes consist of the rapid implementation of a
large number of small projects drawn from a limited
range of eligible project types and using standardised technologies. There is neither time nor
talent available for formal benefit-cost analysis of
each project, and efforts to do so will result in
costly delays in approval and implementation.
Scarce technical and administrative skills can be
better used to solve the practical problems of
implementation, coordination with cooperating
ministries, and inclusion of public works projects
in a coherent system of local planning.

    On a macroeconomic level, it would therefore
theoretically be possible to analyse, through a
macro-modeling linear programming exercise, the
effect of a rural works programme on the national

economy. Such an approach was suggested in a study of "Promotion Nationale" in Morocco. [4] Given the realities of data limitation and the relatively small size of most rural works programmes, it would appear more practical to limit evaluation efforts to the project level.

Do Distributive and Development Goals Conflict?

Given the multiple objectives of employment, asset creation and redistribution both in the construction and operating phases, must there be important sacrifices of one goal to achieve the other? As suggested in Chapter Three, there are differences between categories of projects in relation to each of these goals. The differences, particularly in relation to distributive goals, are strongly influenced by socio-economic variables such as land holding patterns and access to social infra-structure assets. Directly productive projects, partly due to ease of measurement, show the highest economic returns and are effective creators of employment in both the construction and the operating phases. As pointed out in the previous chapter, there are numerous ways to increase the proportion of operating phase benefits that will go to target groups, for both directly productive and economic infrastructure assets, although the patterns of land ownership will remain the basic determinant of the distribution. Accepting the fact that these programmes will have only moderately redistributive effects in the absence of basic structural reforms, there is a broad consistency between employment, developmental and distributive goals in a programme of diversified projects. Important sacrifices of one goal are not necessary to obtain reasonable levels of other objectives. A possible short-term exception exists in the form of crisis relief programmes, where it may be necessary to place maximum weight on construction phase employment. But even in such cases, increased efforts can be made to relate the programme, as it continues, to other developmental aims, while preserving high levels of labour intensity.

Programme Size

What yardsticks are available as guides for

determining the optimal size of a programme? In theory, an upper limit might be set by the estimated extent of rural unemployment. Such an approach is unrealistic for a number of reasons, As pointed out in Chapter Two, many members of the programme's target group cannot be reached because they will not or cannot accept employment of this sort. Other constraints include shortages of administrative and technical skills to mount a programme of massive size, a possible shortage of eligible projects of sufficiently high quality in the regions where they are required, the political realities of the competitive struggle for allocation in the light of other pressing national needs, and the gross financial constraints that would be encountered by any programme attempting to "solve" in the short run the problem of large-scale rural unemployment. By international standards, any programme absorbing as much as 10% of rural unemployment must be considered large, and most programmes fall well below that level.

1. **What are the financial implications of programmes of typical size?** Table 4.1 shows the percentage of GDP represented by programme expenditures in 21 programmes in 14 countries. [5] The GDP proportion tends to understate total costs since official figures usually exclude local and regional contributions, and those portions of administrative costs that are included in other departmental budgets. The range of understatement is generally in the area of 10 per cent to 25 per cent.

In terms of programme purposes, long-term employment programmes make the greatest claims on resources, reflecting the size and visibility of the problem of such structural unemployment, and the decision in two of the three such programmes to pay the standard government wage for urban workers. The income augmenting programmes show the greatest range in GDP proportions. Three programmes, Bangladesh, Morocco and Tunisia, all represented expenditures of more than 0.5 per cent of GDP. The four low-cost infrastructure programmes, while they may have important local effects, were extremely small in relation to their national economies.

The Tunisian is an extreme case. At its peak in the early 1960s, expenditures on Lutte Contre le Sous Developpement (LCSD) totalled almost 5 per cent of the GDP and represented almost 24 per cent gross fixed capital formation. Rural works expenditures on this level are clearly insupportable for extended periods and reflect the absence of alternatives available to Tunisia at that time, a situation which hopefully does not now exist elsewhere. Since 1963, this programme has been much smaller and it seems unlikely that future rural works programmes will reach a comparable size.

Working from Table 4.1, the following figures suggest the cost in relation to GDP of providing one day of employment for each labour force member (using government labour force estimates for the early 1970s):

Bangladesh	0.38%	Korea	0.14%
India-CSRE	.15	Mauritius	.24
India-Relief	.15	Morocco	.19
India-DPAP	.25	Pakistan	.63
Afghanistan	.39	Tunisia	.12
Indonesia	.27	Trinidad	.34
Jamaica	.40		

An unweighted average of these figures is 0.27 per cent. These figures are purely illustrative, and take no account of multiplier or other effects connected with large-scale wage payments. Assume that un- and underemployment in a country is estimated at 15 per cent of the labour force. To "solve" such an unemployment problem on the basis of the average cost obtained above would require an expenditure of approximately 10 per cent of GDP. Even the absorption of 10 per cent of the estimated unemployment would cost 1 per cent of GDP, a level approached or exceeded by only four of the countries shown in Table 4.1.

2. What is the tendency shown by programme size over time? Table 4.2 gives details for the five income augmenting programmes for which statistics are available. With the exception of Morocco, the programmes, all of which are of the income supplementing category, show a tendency to decline. In addition to programme-specific factors, the tendency to decrease in size reflects the stabilisation of programme expectations after the initial enthusiasm of the beginning years, and may also reflect the ending of PL 480 support in some countries and its decreasing availability and higher cost (sharing of ocean freight, etc.) in other countries.

Table 4.1.--Relative Size of Special Rural Works Programmes in Terms of Employment and Resources

Country	Programme	Period	Worker-days of employment per member of labour force	Programme expenditure as a per cent of GDP
			(annual average)	
Relief programmes				
Afghanistan	Provincial Development	1971-72	1.1	0.43
Brazil	DNOCS	1958	14.0[a]	0.38[b]
India	Security Relief	1969-74	2.2	0.33
Long-term employment programmes				
Jamaica	Special Employment	1974[c]	3.5	1.4
Mauritius	Relief Workers' Programme	1974	6.0[d]	0.76[d]
	Travail pour Tous	1974	4.0[d]	1.12[d]
	Rural Development Project	1974	5.2[d]	1.76[d]
Trinidad-Tobago	Special Works Programme PM's Special Programme	1970-71	2.6	0.89
Income-augmenting programmes				
Bangladesh	The Works Programme	1962-68	1.5	0.57
India	Crash Scheme for Rural Employment	1972	1.0	0.15
	Drought Prone Areas	1970-72	0.2	

Table 4.1, continued

Country	Programme	Period	Worker-days of employment per member of labour force	Programme expenditure as a per cent of GDP
Indonesia	Kabupaten	1972-73	0.9	0.24
South Korea	Self-help Work Programme	1964-70	2.9	0.41
Morocco	Promotion Nationale	1961-72	3.1	0.60
Pakistan	Rural Works Programme	1964-72	0.3	0.19
Tunisia	LCSD	1959-69	20.7	2.40
Low-cost infrastructure programmes				
Columbia	Pico y Pala	1972-73	0.2	0.05
Indonesia	Padat Karya	1973	0.4[d]	0.03[d]
	Desa	1973	--	0.12[d]
Ethiopia	Tigre Development Organisation	1971-72	0.2[e]	0.01

a Estimated regional figure.
b National
c Proposed at the time.
d Estimated.
e Based on the labour force among the provincial rural population.

43

Table 4.2.--Trends in Programme Size Over Time

	1960	1961	1962	1963	1964	1965	1966	1967	1968	1969	1970	1971	1972	1973
Bangladesh (East Pakistan)														
Worker-days/member of labour force				2.8	2.8	2.8	0.9	1.1	0.9					
Programme expenditure/GDP (in %)				0.52	0.98	0.72	0.39	0.42	0.67					
Programme expenditure/development budget (in %)				9.1	13.3	8.3	6.2	6.7	7.1	5.7	5.4	4.9	5.3	3.2
Pakistan (West Pakistan)														
Worker-days/member of labour force					0.45	0.43	0.25	0.24	0.23	0.22	0.21	0.17	0.17	
Programme expenditure/GDP (in %)					0.34	0.37	0.32	0.06	0.16	0.15	0.16			
Programme expenditure/development budget (in %)					5.6	4.5	5.6	0.1	2.5	2.2	3.0			
South Korea														
Worker-days/member of labour force		3.2			2.3	3.3	2.9	3.2	2.6	3.1	1.4			
Programme expenditure/GDP (in %)		1.6			0.41	0.55	0.61	0.45	0.36	0.27	0.20			
Programme expenditure/development budget (in %)		20.2			11.3	12.8	13.6	7.9	5.8	2.8	2.8	1.9	1.4	
Morocco														
Worker-days/member of labour force		3.0	2.9	1.0	3.1	2.8	4.2	3.8	3.6	3.6	3.8	3.1	2.1	
Programme expenditure/GDP (in %)		0.43	0.72	0.55	0.57	0.48	0.83	0.75	0.62	0.59	0.64	0.50	0.24	
Programme expenditure/gross fixed capital formation (in %)		3.3	6.0	4.2	4.6	3.9	6.2	4.8	4.3	3.8	3.7	3.1		
Tunisia														
Worker-days/member of labour force	23.9	42.1	43.3	25.9	20.2	18.3	11.4	14.0	11.2	12.3	11.0	5.5	4.9	
Programme expenditure/GDP (in %)	2.9	4.6	4.9	2.9	2.1	2.0	1.6	1.9	1.4	1.5				
Programme expenditure/gross fixed capital formation (in %)	16.5	24.7	24.0	14.9	9.0	7.4	6.2	7.9	6.5	6.7				

3. <u>Claim on Resources</u>. It is clear that any programme attempting to make a substantial impact on unemployment will require a heavy commitment of government resources -- the average for the three programmes in Table 4.2 for which such information is available is 6.4 per cent of the development budget. Moreover, none of these programmes would be classified as "large" in terms of their overall impact on unemployment. <u>If a country's development budget represented 10 per cent of GDP, then a programme reaching 10 per cent of unemployment, on the assumption above, would also absorb 10 per cent of the development budget. On a realistic fiscal basis, continued funding at this level will mean severe competition with other development programmes, and will require a strong level of political and bureaucratic support.</u>

Inflationary Potential

What is the potential inflationary effect on wage good prices, particularly basic foodstuffs, of a large rural works programme? It is sometimes argued that in the absence of commodity wage payments a large-scale rural works programme will run the risk of causing serious price inflation, thus reducing or perhaps eliminating the anticipated benefits to target groups. The question is certainly valid when one sees programmes that absorb substantial portions of national resources, as with Tunisia in the 1960s and the level of operations for Mauritius in 1974.

To take an extreme case, one can look at Tunisia's LCSD programme for 1966. In that year the programme provided the equivalent of over eleven days of employment for each member of the labour force and represented about 1.5% of GDP. If the entire programme cost were raised by taxes in urban areas and spent entirely on labour and materials supplied by rural households, net consumption of cereals, using 1966 prices and government income elasticities, would rise by about 9,000 tonnes. This represents only 1.5% of total Tunisian cereal output in 1966. [6]

Had the entire programme been financed externally, implying no decrease in urban consumption, the increase in total demand for cereals would be about 13,000 tonnes, or 2.2 per cent of Tunisian cereal output. This suggests that on a macro-basis the increase in demand for wage goods resulting from a rural works programme of this size in relation to GDP is likely to be slight, and thus that the programme's inflationary effect should be small.

In the early 1960s this programme was much larger. In 1962 for example, when programme expenditures were almost 5 per cent of GDP, the net additional demand for cereal grains on the same basis as above should have been about 31,000 tonnes or 6.3 per cent of total production. Depending on the proportion of output that is marketed, a programme of this size might well have strong inflationary effects in the absence of food aid or foreign food purchases. However, such a large programme is exceptional.

A similar calculation can be made for Pakistan's Rural Works Programme based on average expenditures for the years 1963-71. During these years the programme expenditures represented 0.21 per cent of GDP, making it one of the smaller, but still representative income augmenting programmes. Using demand elasticities from a 1968-69 consumer expenditure survey, and assuming that all programme funds came from middle and upper-income urban families and all expenditures went to poor rural families, the greatest net change would have been 0.2 per cent in the demand for cereals, Assuming complete external finance, with no reduction in urban consumption, the increase in cereal demand would have been approximately 0.3 per cent.

Given the size of most income augmenting programmes, there should be no important wage good constraints or strong inflationary pressure on food prices. However, such problems may be faced by income augmenting programmes if they should reach the size of Tunisia's LCSD in the early 1960s or by others which concentrate their activities in a small geographical area. In Maharashtra, for example, where in 1973-74 scarcity relief works generated an estimated 290,000,000 worker/days of labour, [7] not only were short-term supply elasticities low, but successive crop failures had produced strong upward pressure on cereal prices. Using the same method as in the Tunisian case, it may be estimated that in this year the scarcity relief programme generated an additional demand for 135,000 tonnes of cereals. Fortunately, good transportation arrangements and outside food supplies offset this potential pressure on prices.

Rapid Implementation versus High Quality Standards

There is frequent tension between the professional engineering desire for high quality standards in the execution of projects and the need for rapid implementation. Questions are sometimes phrased in terms of allocating scarce administrative and technical resources to low priority activities. Sometimes it is suggested that rural works activity should be deferred until all the necessary engineering and supervisory staff are available, in order to assure high quality projects. Both lines of argument are basically negative on the value of projects carried out by labour-intensive rural works programmes, and may mask a bias on the part of the questioner in favour of capital-intensive techniques.

The information summarised earlier on the economic efficiency of well-operated works programmes, and the high priority in most development plans placed on improving living standards for the rural poor, should help to answer these arguments. Training of personnel requires time. If rural works programmes were delayed until fully trained professional staff were in place, years might pass without action.

Much can be done to start programmes before all the desired technical staff have been trained and still achieve a satisfactory level of economic efficiency. The use of a brief pilot programme is discussed in Chapter Five. There are frequently administrative and technical capacities outside of the government bureaucracy which can be tapped by a rural works programme. This is particularly true in Asian countries where traditional arrangements exist for communal labour-intensive activities. Grass roots knowledge is available and can be utilised in a rural works programme, particularly if it is organised on a participatory decentralised basis. An innovative approach, coupled with a continuing effort to simplify and standardise procedures, can locate many substitutes for scarce technical skills and extend the available talent pool to permit the most rapid expansion of implementation consistent with minimum acceptable quality standards.

Appropriate Wage Rates

Levels of worker compensation have an important effect on programme performance. Wage rates on

public works projects should approximate market rates and should be based on an incentive system for labour efficiency. Achieving reasonable labour intensity and paying wage rates that approximate market rates will ensure positive distributive arrangements in the construction phase of projects.
        Table 4.3 summarises the mode and level of wage payments in fourteen countries in the late 1960s and early 1970s. The trends observed then were clearly away from commodity wages and toward a wage scale that approaches the existing agricultural wage. Since the data of Table 4.3 were released, Tunisia and Morocco have gone to a straight cash payment approximating the official minimum agricultural wage.

Misuse of Funds

        How can corruption and misuse of funds be kept within tolerable limits? Rural works programmes involve local or regional decisions on hiring, purchasing, awarding contracts, and selecting and locating projects, and it is at these levels, rather than at the centre, that misuse of funds is likely to occur. Though firm data are obviously not available, it appears that financial corruption in most of the programmes studied does not divert a high proportion of benefits away from intended target groups. In two cases (Northeast Brazil and Bangladesh in the early 1970s) where widespread misuse of funds did reduce programme effectiveness, political influences were clearly involved. Systems of reporting, public information, etc., that will help reduce possible corruption are suggested in Chapter Five.

The Role of Women

        Women have played a very limited part in rural works programmes. Only one programme, Jamaica's, makes special reference to providing employment for women, but to date relatively few have been employed. Many reasons are cited for excluding or limiting the participation of women, ranging from physical incapacity for manual labour to religious, social, caste and tribal view on the proper role of women in the economy. There is evidence that these views may be exaggerated and that there are important reasons for attempting to include women

Major Issues in Rural Works Programmes

Table 4.3.--Wage Rates in Public Works Programmes

Country	Programme	Mode of payment	Wage scale
Afghanistan	Provincial Development	Food/cash	Approximately 1/2 agricultural wage
Bangladesh	Works Programme	Cash	Agricultural market rate
Brazil	DNOCS	Cash	Unknown
Columbia	Pico y Pala	Cash	Incentive wage higher than agricultural wage
Ethiopia	Food for Work	Food/cash	Approximately 2/3 agricultural wage
India	Crash Scheme	Cash	Slack season rate
	Drought Prone Areas	Cash	Variable
Indonesia	Kabupaten Programme	Cash	Agricultural rate
	Padat Karya	Food/cash	One-half agricultural rate
Jamaica	Special Employment	Cash	Government minimum wage
Mauritius	Travail pour Tous	Cash	78% of government minimum wage
	Rural Development	Cash	78% of government minimum wage
Morocco	Promotion Nationale	Food/cash	Approximately 3/4 agricultural rate
Pakistan	Rural Works	Cash	Agricultural rate
South Korea	Self-help Work	Food/cash	Approximately 2/3 agricultural rate
Trinidad-Tobago	Prime Minister's Special Works	Cash	Government minimum wage
Tunisia	Lutte Contre le Sous Developpement	Food/cash	Approximately 3/4 agricultural rate

much more fully.

In Bangladesh, a Muslim country where purdah is widely observed, the assumption of the rural works programme was that women would not be willing or permitted to participate in projects. None ever did, and those associated with the programme assumed this to be a situation that would continue indefinitely. However, in 1974-75, during the acute food shortages, one local government decided, together with UNICEF, to hire "destitute" women to carry out agricultural projects. In part the work consisted of establishing small gardens, but it also involved digging irrigation and drainage channels which entailed heavy earth-moving. When the crisis period was over, UNICEF announced its intention to withdraw support on the assumption that with reduced need, the women would no longer be willing to do this type of work. Contrary to expectation, the women demanded that the programme be continued and expanded. These requests were granted and the programme has steadily grown. In addition, it has provided the organisational focus which enabled the women to begin a functional educational programme.

This experience suggests that the assumptions about women's disinterest in programmes may be incorrect and ought to be tested. In addition, there is growing evidence in the literature of development related to family size, nutrition and family health which suggests that women's work may alter their behaviour in important ways and may lead to reduced family size and improved nutrition and health practices in the home. This will be particularly true if programmes such as functional education are built upon women's participation in rural works.

Encouraging the participation of women will require special efforts and the modification of some programme designs or the establishment of parallel activities. The potential benefits however seem to justify such efforts as may be required to incorporate women in rural works programmes.

The Scope for Urban Works

Existing programmes have concentrated their activities in rural areas. Where programmes do operate in towns and cities, they are generally unadapted extensions of rural programmes, and little attention is paid to the distinguishing characteristics of urban unemployment or the special needs of

the urban environment. In only one case, that of
Jamaica, was specific attention given to the problem
of urban unemployment when public works activity was
started. As shown in Table 4.4, almost half of the
countries' programmes gave no evidence of having any
urban projects.

Part of the bias against urban public works
stems from the location of unemployment in the
countries adopting these programmes. With the
exception of Mauritius and Jamaica, the countries
listed in Table 4.4 have an average of only 8.7 per
cent of their population in urban areas. For these
countries unemployment is primarily a rural
phenomenon.

While the magnitudes of unemployment are much
larger in rural areas, rates of unemployment and
rates of population growth are usually higher in
towns and cities. There is a concern, both economic
and political, with the consequences of rapid urbanisation in most developing countries. The lack of
an urban focus may be attributed in part to a desire
not to stimulate additional in-migration to cities.
Slowing the rate of rural-urban migration was an
explicit objective of Pakistan's Rural Works
Program, Morocco's Promotion Nationale, and
Indonesia's Kabupaten Program, and it is an implicit
objective in such programs as Tunisia's LCSD and
India's Scarcity Relief operation. However, the
available evidence suggests that it is easier to
encourage migration to cities by increasing urban
employment opportunities and raising wages than to
curb it by improving employment conditions in rural
areas. [8] While the evidence is not conclusive, it
can be inferred that rural public works programmes
are unlikely to have an appreciable effect on rural-
urban migration and that the introduction of urban
public works might increase migration flows.

Migration issues aside, the evidence suggests
that conventional public works have not performed
well and are not well suited to urban areas. In
Jamaica's Impact Works, the one programme with a
substantial urban component, productivity has been
notoriously low. Evidence from the other programmes
with urban components, while not definitive, shows
lower percentages of programme expenditures on wages
for unskilled labour and lower productivity than in
rural projects, as well as the construction of non-
essential assets.

The characteristics of urban unemployment imply
that if a public works programme is to ensure an
adequate income for its employees, more scarce

Table 4.4--Percentage of Rural Works Funds Allocated to Urban Areas and Per Cent of Population Residing in Urban Areas

Country	Period	Types of urban projects	Proportion of total funds for urban areas (per cent)	Urban as a proportion of total population (per cent)	Comments
Bangladesh	1963-68	Roads, community centres	8	5.6	Funds allocated to municipal councils limited to the same activities as in the rural areas.
Jamaica	1974-76	Housing improvement, clean-up	40 (Kingston)	37.4	Previous programmes stressed urban clean up.
Mauritius	1971-74	Industrial estate and housing site preparation	9	44	For schools, roads and artisan workshops, no urban distinction is available. Inclusion of these would increase the urban component.
Morocco	1961-72	Sewers, housing, drainage	11	18.9	All in small towns.
South Korea:					
NCS	1961-63	Drainage, sewers, redistricting, roads,	7]	]	
Self-help	1964-68	housing, site preparation	6.8]	22]	
Tunisia	1960-70	Housing	10+	15.6	All in small towns. No official statistics distinguish urban expenditure.

SOURCE: Figures for urban activity from programme reports. Data on urban population are for 1960 because expenditure figures are for 1960 except for Jamaica. Data from Taylor and Hudson, World Handbook of Political and Social Indicators, New Haven, 1972, and for Bangladesh, Jamaica and Mauritius from national statistical publications.

NOTE: Programmes in the following countries gave no evidence of having urban projects (figures in parentheses are the percentage of the population residing in urban areas): Afghanistan (2.7), Ethiopia (2.7), India (9.0), Indonesia (9.7) and Pakistan (9.7).

resources will be needed than in rural areas:
-       urban unemployment tends to be open and
year-round, and thus a programme to alleviate it
must provide regular long-term jobs from which
employees can realise a full income;
-       urban costs of living are generally higher
than rural, and if public works employees are to be
permitted reasonable consumption levels, the cost
per worker day of employment created will be higher
than in rural areas; and
-       the urban unemployed are typically
heterogeneous, from a wide range of backgrounds and
with a wide range of skills and education levels.
Designing a programme for people of diverse
capacities and skills is highly demanding of
administrative resources, a capacity always in short
supply.
        All of these factors mean that an effective
urban public works programme must differ from a
rural programme. There is little scope in urban
areas for the large scale labour-intensive earth-
moving work that characterises rural projects.
There is a great need for programmes to provide
social infrastructure to benefit low income urban
groups, but such programmes are difficult to
organise and to administer, and more difficult to
defend on a benefit/cost basis. There is a need for
research and small experimental pilot programmes to
find ways in which works programmes can be
specifically adapted to urban environments. We
conclude that without a specific urban design,
public works programmes should remain rural.

Consistency with Other Programmes

        Even a relatively large works programme will be
unable to solve the problems of substantial rural
unemployment by itself. Clearly a major improvement
in the employment situation will require other
government policies that promote employment creation
and reinforce the works programme.
        In only two of the existing countries which
have rural work programmes does the policy mix
clearly favour labour absorption. In all other
cases the blend is neutral at best and tends to work
against employment creation. Unless greater policy
coherence is obtained, rural works programmes can
continue to provide helpful supplements to
disadvantaged groups, and will continue to create
economically useful assets in the countryside, but

they will be marginal in their impact on the
underlying problems of employment and poverty.
    There are many policy areas and programmes that
affect employment. They can be grouped conveniently
as outlined below. Administrators should think
about each of these areas to see if existing
policies are consistent with public works:
    1.   Agricultural mechanisation. Do government
programmes encourage substitution of machinery for
labour in agriculture? Are farmers offered
financial incentives to mechanise? Is the impact of
extension services conducive to labour displacement?
    2.   Manufacturing technology. Is there a
capital bias in the incentives offered to foreign or
domestic investors? Do domestic interest rates
subsidise capital? Are special incentives offered
for labour-intensive investments? Is there a
sharply dualistic wage structure?
    3.   Foreign exchange rate. Is this consis-
tently overvalued so as to attract capital-
intensive investment and imports of labour-replacing
machinery?
    4.   Pricing policies. Do agricultural
policies produce incentives by offering protection
against price declines or providing profitable
prices? Are subsidies or special incentives offered
for labour-intensive production either for domestic
markets or for export? Are agricultural inputs made
available at rates and in programmes that encourage
their application in a labour-intensive manner?
    5.   Other government programmes. Is there an
efficient small farmer credit programme? Are
extension workers trained and conditioned to
advocate labour-intensive techniques? Are rural
infrastructure and agricultural development
programmes outside the public works programme
designed to promote labour-intensive practices?
Does the pattern of tax incidence and the rural-
urban terms of trade improve or worsen rural living
standards?

Broadening Participation in National Development

    For most countries, a rural works programme
will broaden participation in national development
programmes substantially. The capacity to stimulate
participation in many different forms is seen by
most, including the authors, as one of the real
advantages of rural works. In designing the administrative system to govern such a programme, full

consideration must be given to what forms of participation are encouraged and how that participation is structured. The administrator must make the following critical decisions which will determine the degree of participation invoked:

1. What role should be assigned to local government in project decisions, work supervision and planning? Involving local government bodies in this aspect of the programme is an important way of obtaining participation and of developing local capacity.

2. Who should participate in decision making for project selection? Allowing the local community to participate in this aspect of the programme makes them much more aware of what is going on and also gives them a "stake" in the programme.

3. Should public information as to amounts of money and accomplishments be used as a means of checking on misuse? This too will make the local populace much more aware of what is going on and involve them in the programme.

4. Should employment opportunities be spread as widely as possible within a target group? One effect of a seasonal programme is that it spreads a limited wage fund more broadly.

5. Should target groups be organised formally through cooperatives or small farmer/farm labourer associations as a means of increasing and channeling their participation?

The programme administrator should be aware that programmes that have invoked participation have incurred political interference much more frequently than non-participatory ones. Participation inevitably has political ramifications. If a regime sees that participation generated through rural works is building rural support for the government, as a successful programme inevitably will, the programme will be assured strong political support. In East Pakistan, this type of support was one of the programme's great assets in its early years, but it eventually became a crippling liability, as efforts to use the programme for direct political patronage eroded its impact.

Other programmes that have invoked participation, such as the Korean Self Help Work Programme, or the Workers' Brigades in Ghana, have generally not survived a major change of government or have done so only in an altered form. On the other hand, programmes which have not invoked participation, and as a result may have achieved much less in the way of mobilising the populace or creating new capacity for development at local levels, have had a more stable history. Promotion Nationale in Morocco has been an administratively managed programme with a minimum of citizen participation and its performance has been one of the most stable over time. Despite these drawbacks, the authors feel that the benefits of participatory programmes are greater than those achieved when minimum participation is generated. Non-participatory programmes frequently fail to generate local capacity for other development efforts or to achieve their potential multiplier effects. The long term employment programmes, which are both centralised and non-participatory, have proven to be high-cost and inefficient. As a result, broadening participation is recommended and in later sections means will be suggested of reducing the dangers of political interference through adjustments in scale, appropriate procedures, and integration with other rural development efforts.

Decentralisation and Levels of Responsibility

Most rural works programmes share a basic organisational characteristic: work sites are numerous and scattered. This inevitably requires some decentralisation of administration. The issue of which levels of government should have responsibility for implementing a rural works programme is a complex one, and international experience varies widely. In Mauritius the Development Works Corporation, a national agency, hires all the programme workers on its year-round payroll, decides on projects, and then assigns workers to them. Indonesia, Pakistan and Bangladesh have substantially decentralised programmes, with a basic framework decided at the centre and implementing authority delegated to the local bodies. Pakistan's decision to place responsibility at the district level ultimately resulted in the programme becoming biased toward the needs of large farmers, and not the majority of the population. It is essential that the programme designer carefully consider the groups who will influence the decision makers and ascertain that such influence is consistent with programme objectives. Decentralisation follows one of two patterns. It can be bureaucratic, with project decisions and implementation carried out through existing departments, or participatory, with the public sharing in the decision making through councils or local representative bodies. The former approach may simplify adherence to centrally defined guidelines; the latter approach offers the possibility of greater public interest and mobilisation in support of the programme, but carries with it the risks of excessive politicalisation and divergence from standard procedure. The appropriate choice in a given country depends on the relative competence, honesty and staffing of local government and local administration. The authors feel that if local conditions permit, some participatory decentralisation is highly desirable. A number of countries, including Bangladesh and Indonesia have discovered unused and unrecognised capacity at the local level. It is important to develop and exploit these capabilities.

Although it may seem paradoxical, the most important requirement for effective decentralised administration, particularly of a participatory nature, is strong central control. Such control is needed to enforce the adherence to national priorities and procedures, and to ensure that all interests of target groups are protected at the local level.

Decisions concerning the form and extent of decentralised administration depend on the importance attached to mobilisation goals, the relative honesty, competence and staffing of local government and local bureaus of central ministries, the existence and competence of local representative councils, and the degree to which they reflect the interests of the intended target groups as opposed to those of local elites or entrenched special interest groups.

An interesting dimension of the centralisation question is its relationship to foreign aid. Fourteen programmes were ranked on a scale of decentralisation on the basis of the level of government at which critical programme decisions were made. Of the seven most centralised, six were supported by aid. This suggests that aid donors may impose requirements for accountability and reporting that favour centralisation or may even have an outright preference for more centralised programmes. While this should not be interpreted as an argument against aid for rural works programmes, it should warn the administrator that special vigilance may be needed to make sure that the desired level of decentralisation is obtained.

NOTES

1. See, for example, International Bank for Reconstruction and Development Staff Working Paper No. 172, January 1974; Deepak Lal, "Men and Machines: A Philippines Case Study of Labour-Capital Substitution in Road Construction," International Labour Office, Geneva, mimeographed, 1973; and ILO, "Roads and Redistribution: A Social Cost-Benefit Study of Labour Intensive Road Construction Methods in Iran," International Labour Office, Geneva, 1973, Chapter IV.

2. Hussain, Syed Mushtaq, "Strategy of Agricultural Development with special reference to Pakistan," Pakistan Institute of Development Economics, Karachi, mimeo, 1970.

3. Checci and Co., Food for Peace: An Evaluation of PL480 Title II, Washington D.C.; 1972, Vol. K, a study contracted for by USAID. See also Government of Indonesia, Manpower Department, Labour Intensive Research Team, Labour Intensive Research in Java and Madura, mimeographed, 1972.

4. Andriamananjara.

5. The single measure of programme size in relation to GDP was chosen to facilitate comparison. Ratios of programme expenditure to development budget, total government expenditure and capital formation, which would give additional insights into the importance of public works programmes in their national settings, were discarded due to differing definitions and incomplete data.

6. Figures on production and programme costs are taken from Grissa Abdessatar, Agricultural Policies and Employment: Case Study of Tunisia, OECD, Paris, 1973.

7. Authors' estimate. Official figures for employment generation are not accumulated.

8. See Harris, John R. and Michael P. Todaro, "Migration, Unemployment and Development: A Two-Sector Analysis," The American Economic Review, Vol. LX, No. 1., March 1970, pp. 126-142; Bank Staff Working Paper, International Migration in LDC's: A Survey of the Literature, September 1975: Kraft, J.D., "Slum Development in South and Southeast Asia," paper delivered at the Conference on Town and City Planning, Colombo, 1971; Rosser, C., Urbanisation in India, International Urbanisation Survey, the Ford Foundation, New York, n.d.

Chapter Five

ORGANISATION AND OPERATION

The details of organising and operating a rural
works programme are just as important as the
programme's concept and design. This chapter moves
from basic concepts of design to the detailed
organisation and operation of a programme.

The programme administrators must understand
that the original design will condition the way the
programme develops. They must think carefully about
the objectives and techniques to be used to achieve
these objectives. Directions from the centre will
be interpreted and applied by many people in the
field, most of whom will have limited knowledge of
overall programme aims. In order to minimise misun-
derstandings and unforeseen results, it is essential
that instructions are expressed in simple unam-
biguous terms. This chapter provides detailed
guidelines for the actual administration of
programmes. In using these guidelines the administrator must be aware of the need to modify them to
fit a particular situation.

New Systems of Administration Required

As indicated in Chapter One, rural works are in
many respects a unique type of development
programme. They require organisation at many
levels of government. They frequently involve the
participation and cooperation of non-government
people. As a result, they require forms of
organisation and concepts that may not be familiar
to the government officer. The starting point for
developing an administrative system is a full
understanding of the programme's objectives. A
second step is thinking through what agencies and
what levels of government have the capacity to share

in administering the programme. Central government
control has not provided an adequate basis around
which to design these programmes in the past. The
administrator must therefore consider the capacity
for implementation which is available outside the
central government. This means that there will be a
need to develop new procedures and activities, with
relatively untested groups taking on new responsibilities. In innovating, the administrator must be
aware that it is necessary to test new procedures in
pilot programmes on limited areas before committing
a whole programme. He must ensure that there is
good communication and feedback in the programme,
establish a system to generate critical data indicators of performance, and have a continuing and
objective evaluation system which will highlight
problem areas or ineffective procedures. In
summary, the administrative system must be innovative, must ensure good internal communication, and
be highly flexible.

Alternative Implementing Agencies

Systems for national level administration of
rural works programmes can be placed in three broad
categories:

1.   Special Executive or Autonomous Agencies--
When programmes are established on a private basis,
frequently with the specific endorsement of the head
of state, they are often located in the executive
offices or in a special autonomous agency. So long
as they retain the backing of the head of state,
such arrangements give a programme great power.
However, if there is a change of government or if
the head of state loses interest, programmes administered in this way find themselves relatively weak
and outside the mainstream of power. Their special
status frequently engenders the animosity of regular
line agencies. If the power conferred by the head
of state is removed, the regular agencies can
quickly reduce the role and effectiveness of such an
agency.

2.   Within Regular Ministries or
Administrative Hierarchies--This is a logical place
to locate programmes, and over the long term the
most effective. The programme is incorporated in
the regular procedures of government and occupies a
relatively stable place in the government hierarchy.
Another pattern is followed in India, where state
level governments have responsibility for implemen-

ting programmes and the regular civil service field officers are used. This too seems a relatively effective arrangement. The one exception is where a rural works programme is a peripheral part of the activities of a ministry, in which case it is apt to be weak and neglected.

3. Programmes Administered Jointly by More than One Agency--This pattern exists in several of the large programmes: Tunisia, Indonesia and Jamaica. Lacking an existing ministry into which the programme logically fits, a regime will create an inter-ministerial committee to give the programme overall direction and to supervise implementation by a number of agencies. While this arrangement appears to have the advantage of cabinet level support and would seem to provide access to multiple skills, it can also lead to a situation in which rural works become everybody's priority. On balance the most reliable form of organisation is one which places responsibility for the programme in an existing ministry at the national level, preferably one which has responsibilities for local government in the rural areas.

At the field level the choices are more difficult. Some relevant considerations have been mentioned in the discussion of participation and decentralisation. The four most common implementing agencies are: central government agencies acting through their own officials, government administrative officers already posted at the local level, local elective bodies such as local councils, and private contractors. Many countries use some combination of these agencies. The decision should reflect the strengths and weaknesses of each potential implementing agency in the particular environment. For example, in East Pakistan, contractors were rejected because of their traditionally corrupt relations with government in carrying out projects. Instead, local elective councils shared implementation responsibility with a generalist administrative officer at the county level. In Indonesia exactly the opposite was true. Local councils were considered unreliable, while contractors functioned with general competence and honesty. In this case local governments did the programme planning, but the contractors did the actual implementation.

The use of private contractors in implementing projects raises special questions. Contractors are attractive for administrative simplicity and they provide access to existing supervisory and engi-

neering capacities. The disadvantages can include a
tendency to move toward capital-intensive technologies, the use of imported labour rather than local
residents, and in some cases an increased risk of
financial corruption, politicisation, and a lessened
ability to use the programme to supplement seasonal
employment patterns. In general, the use of
contractors should be discouraged in the absence
of compelling reasons for employing them.

The criteria to be used in deciding on the best
implementing arrangements should include the
following:

1. Does the agency have the administrative
    capacity to carry out programmes?
2. Does the agency have the technical
    capacity to implement projects?
3. Is there past experience that demonstrates
    these capacities?
4. What agencies have been traditionally
    responsible in the use of government
    funds?
5. Which agencies have contact with the local
    population and can be effective in
    mobilising participation in both the
    planning process and the project
    implementation stage?

With these criteria, it is possible to make
some judgement as to the most appropriate local
implementing agency.

Estimating Needs

Before a public works programme is started, it
is important to determine in general terms the needs
that can be met by such a programme, the sorts of
projects that should be considered, and the desirable forms of organisation based on bureaucratic or
governmental capabilities. These general guidelines
can best be determined by a micro survey of a
limited number of representative villages or rural
areas. If the rural economy includes distinct
regional variations in the basic parameters that
influence programme effectiveness, such as agricultural systems, a series of studies will be needed to
highlight the differences between regions. Such
analyses are in effect feasibility studies and
should be based on close analysis of representative
areas, involving consultation with village and local

leaders in order to obtain a clear picture of the
most pressing needs and problems.

Developing Tentative Programme Outlines

As a result of these detailed local studies,
tentative programme outlines should be developed,
including profiles of eligible project types,
appropriate technologies, timing schedules to take
advantage of seasonal patterns, and an estimate of
the appropriate scale of the programme, based on the
extent of unemployment, the relative incidence of
poverty, and the apparent availability of potential
projects. These guidelines are at this stage still
tentative and will be refined in the next stage,
which is the establishment of a pilot programme.

Pilot Programmes

In all rural works programmes except crisis
situations which require immediate action, a pilot
programme is essential. The purpose of the pilot
programme is to test the ideas developed as a result
of the micro studies and make necessary adjustments
before a full scale national or regional programme
is launched. A vital part of the pilot programme is
a continuing evaluation to take advantage of
feedback in such areas as refinement of operating
manuals, reporting systems, suggested technologies,
and implementation. It also provides the opportunity to test local capabilities. The capacity of
local government institutions at various levels, the
feasibility of particular technologies, and the
ability of local groups to employ them are examples
of issues that need to be explored through a pilot
project. If possible, the pilot programme should be
closely evaluated by a research institute, rural
development academy or university in addition to the
bureaucratic organisation that will be responsible
for the operation of the programme.
The pilot programme is not an excuse to defer
broader action until all questions are answered and
staffing needs are fully met. A one-year period
should provide the necessary time to make needed
adjustments and prepare for a full scale programme.

Organisation and Operation

Deciding on the Appropriate Size of a Programme

Size has an important bearing on the performance of a rural works programme. Small programmes have frequently functioned much more effectively than large ones. Colombia's Pico y Pala was small and limited to road construction in mountainous areas. In Pakistan, the land development projects of the small-scale Daudzai Rural Development Programme were far more successful than the nationwide People's Works Programme. There are numerous reasons for this:

1. Administrative and technical capacity are always in short supply. Small programmes require fewer administrative and technical inputs than large ones.
2. Small programmes may be tailored more closely to the local environment.
3. Certain problems which may accompany large programmes, such as inflationary pressures, shortages of materials, or constraints on total fiscal resources, do not occur in small programmes.
4. Because of their exposure, large programmes often incur opposition, emanating either from a bureaucracy that sees rural works as a programme operating outside the normal administrative channels, or from local elites who oppose the progress because they cannot control them.

On balance rural works perform better as small programmes, and this manual takes the position that smaller programmes or those integrated with other activities generally have a better chance of success. However, there are some advantages to larger programmes which should be noted and the final decision must be based on specific national needs and capabilities:

1. If employment is widespread, as it is in many countries, a large programme is required to make any significant impact on the problem.
2. There are some economies of scale in administering rural works. Although large programmes may need administrative and technical talents in greater quantities than are available, they may also get more

accomplished for a given input than the
small programmes.

Types of Projects to be Included in the Programme

Since rural works projects are the heart of
the programme, careful consideration must be given
to their selection. Chapter Three has already dealt
with the characteristics of various types of
projects and how they relate to general programme
goals. This section deals with the operational
characteristics of projects and the procedures for
choosing them.

Project selection is crucial. In most
programmes it is desirable to allow this decision to
be made at the local level. Villagers will know
their needs and have a good idea of their capacities
to implement projects. They will also have detailed
knowledge of the local environment, such as high or
low water areas, or the alignments for roads that
will generate the most traffic. Involving the local
community also has the important advantage of mobilising local energies and interest behind the
programme. If it is "their" project the chances of
success, or creating public involvement and of
ensuring maintenance, all become much better.

Experience also suggests that the types of
projects which can be undertaken should be limited.
If the programme administrator wishes to meet
certain national objectives, such as reasonable
economic return, employment creation in the long
term, or some redistribution of income, then it is
important to limit the choice to projects that will
generally achieve these goals. There are also
problems of technical capacity. Projects should not
be authorised until it is known that there are
sufficient skills to implement them effectively.
For example, the East Pakistan programme excluded
irrigation projects from the Works Programme for
five years despite considerable local demand.
During this period the organisation techniques and
technical methods were tested and refined. In 1968
when the techniques had been thoroughly tested,
irrigation works were included in the list of
eligible projects and specific training for local
officials was begun.

The effects of unlimited project choice are
seen in the Peoples Works Programme in Pakistan.
Here the local community had authority to undertake
any type of project it wished. It was impossible to

provide adequate technical help as projects ranged from poultry raising, to playgrounds, latrines and road construction. The results were poor performance in employment creation, many projects that served private rather than public interests and little central control of any sort over programme results.

In general it is desirable to allow substantial local discretion in project selection. However, the types of eligible projects should be limited, clearly defined, and reviewed from time to time to be sure they accurately reflect the priorities of the programme. It may also be necessary to set minimum and maximum quotas on expenditures by project type or groupings of project types.

Chapter Three pointed out the general neglect of consideration of long-term employment creation in project selection. The point is important enough to be re-emphasised here. In deciding on what projects should be included in rural works programmes, attention should be given to long-term employment creation.

The administrator must also be familiar with the operational characteristics of projects. Table 5.1 provides information on three of these characteristics. Column 1 indicates the general frequency of opportunity for various types of projects. Because of special environmental factors such as availability of water, or land that can be reclaimed, there are fewer opportunities for directly productive projects than the other types. Technical skills required in both the construction and operating phase are listed in column 2. Here directly productive projects have requirements that make them more difficult to carry out. Finally, column 3 suggests that the level of maintenance required for each type of project is fairly similar, and that they all require maintenance.

Allocation Systems

Several programmes, including those in Pakistan, Jamaica and Morocco, have developed allocating formulae that give increased allocations to areas of special need, defined in terms of unemployment or poverty indices. Some generally recognised and credible formula is essential. Too many public works programmes have had no official allocating formula, opening the door to undesirable political

Table 5.1.--Operational Characteristics of Different Types of Projects

Type of project	Frequency of opportunity for project	Technical skills required	Maintenance required
Directly productive (Irrigation, drainage, land reclamation, etc.)	Low (Limited by availability of land suitable for such projects)	In construction: high In operation: medium	High (May be the responsibility of beneficiaries)
Economic infrastructure (Roads, conservation, reafforestation, flood control, markets)	High	In construction: low In operation: low	High
Social infrastructure (Schools, community buildings, clinics, etc.)	High	In construction: medium In operation: high (medical personnel, teachers, etc.)	Medium

pressures on the division of funds among regions.

Local Planning for Rural Works

A rural works programme provides an excellent opportunity for decentralised planning, an articulated but unfulfilled objective in many developing countries. The dispersal of projects and the focus on immediate local needs offer a potential framework for basic data collection and the accumulation of information on local conditions and priorities which can be fed upstream and incorporated in regional and national planning processes. The rural works component of a provincial programme in Pakistan has been used as the basis for a "bottom up" approach to integrated rural development, based on a foundation of activist small-farmer organisations. Programmes in Indonesia, Korea and India have served to initiate local planning systems. The most successful model of local planning for public works was that of East Pakistan in the mid-1960s. Each county (approximately 390 square kilometres in area and with a population of about 125,000) prepared a Plan Book providing a phased five-year programme for roads, drainage, flood control, community buildings and local irrigation projects. Organisational and cost estimates were developed for each of the projects, with the active involvement of the county council.

Administratively, rural works must be seen as an opportunity to strengthen local government and attack high priority local problems. In this sense, a rural works programme may constitute the leading edge of a larger approach to rural development. Organising labour for simple, labour-intensive projects is frequently the easiest place to begin organising rural, low-income groups. In time, as competence grows and the organisational techniques are tested and proven, more complex programmes might be undertaken, or rural organisations built out of the works programme structure. For example, public works might start with low-cost road building projects where labour is hired to carry out specific plans that primarily involve earth moving. As organisation is developed, more complicated irrigation projects might be undertaken that involve technically more complicated construction work and which also involve organising farmers to share water and to pay user charges.

Organisation and Operation

        As local governments are strengthened to handle
rural works and local officials are given more
responsibility, the prospects for local organisation
of rural development improve. The use of committees
and participation of the local populace in public
works decisions will develop capacity for other
rural development activities. Programme administrators must constantly be aware of these potential
linkages and be prepared to take advantage of the
new skills, capacities and opportunities that a
rural works programme generates.

Coordination with Other Agencies and Programmes

        The effectiveness of a rural works programme,
particularly in its operating phase, will depend to
a significant degree on the extent to which it is
coordinated with other agricultural and rural
development activities. Directly productive
projects such as minor irrigation works and land
reclamation must be closely coordinated with
agricultural extension services if the potential
benefits are to be realised. The economic and
employment benefits of secondary or farm-to-market
roads will be enhanced if the improved transportation facilities are combined with greater access to
marketing services, public transportation, new
seeds, agricultural credit, government procurement
services, etc. The creation of social infrastructure facilities must be coordinated with a variety
of other governmental services if there are to be
teachers for the new classrooms and medical
personnel and supplies for the new dispensaries.
Rural works programmes produce intermediate goods
and, as such, are dependent on a variety of complementary inputs if potential operating phase benefits
are to be realised. They must therefore be
consciously and formally equipped with mechanisms
for coordination with other departments that provide
related complementary inputs. Formal coordinating
arrangements at the national level can be of some
help in reducing potential inter-agency jealousies
and obstructions, and in providing links in
planning. However, the bulk of the effective coordination efforts must be at the regional and local
levels.
        A related question of coordination which was
mentioned briefly in Chapter Three involves the
allocation of funds to areas of relatively high or
low development potential. The rural works planner

may be faced with difficult choices of allocation
and project siting. Does he attempt to maximise
returns by favouring the advantaged areas, or does
he promote interregional and local equity by
channeling funds to areas with high unemployment
rates, and whose resource base may be inadequate for
their present population? The question is complex,
politically and economically. There is often a
strong political and social desire to spend funds
disproportionately in poorer areas, or at least to
treat regions with equality. The problem of
internal migration is also involved. Reducing
rural-urban, and in some cases rural-rural,
migration is an explicit aim in many rural public
works programmes. Such programmes are often seen as
means of improving living standards and life-chances
of citizens of backward regions and reducing their
desire to migrate. While the effectiveness of a
works programme in this connection is open to considerable doubt, many planners are convinced that it
will succeed. An investment pattern favouring the
economically advantaged areas will undoubtedly
produce high benefit-cost ratios but, on balance,
given the political and distributive aims of these
programmes, it is generally neither realistic nor
desirable.

Implementing rural works programmes in
neglected areas presents special problems of
coordination. Additional efforts to coordinate with
technical ministries will be needed to assure enough
complementary inputs that reasonable levels of
economic efficiency can be reached.

The Use of Project Design and Implementation Manuals

Many local construction projects will require
skills which are not available at the local level.
In some countries the use of simple standardised
manuals provides a solution to this problem. In
East Pakistan a handbook of construction provided
directions ranging from site investigation to
details of construction techniques. There were also
manuals of building, bridge construction, and
standard instructions for irrigation systems. Such
manuals, which present in simple terms the basic
techniques and procedures for construction of a few
authorised types of projects, can do a great deal to
improve the quality of work at the local level.

The Need for an Effective Staff at the National Level

Although rural works programmes are frequently decentralised and implementation personnel are located in the field, it is necessary to have an effective staff at the national level. This staff performs several critical functions in overseeing the programme's implementation. One recurring problem in rural works programmes has been the late release of funds. Sometimes the fault lies with a Ministry of Finance, but in many cases it is simply the failure of the programme staff to realise fully the serious effects of the later release of funds. While there is a limited work season, any funding problem that delays the start of projects is serious. Involvement of local people in the planning process also creates expectations. When these are not met, the credibility of local officials is affected. It is essential that prompt release of funds from the national level be an unbreakable rule of a rural works programme. A member of central staff must also see that reports are submitted on schedule. Once reports are received, they must be analysed promptly. In many programmes the central staff receives reports six to twelve months late and does little with them after they are received. This type of laxity in monitoring field operations is the first step in the process of programme deterioration.

Project Approval

A good degree of decentralisation is desirable. Small projects should be approved and funds committed at the lowest level at which there is adequate engineering capability to provide technical approval and adequate administrative capability for record keeping and supervision of implementation. For larger projects, referral to the next higher level of the bureaucratic or council structure should be adequate, with only the largest projects requiring regional or national approval. It is clearly not desirable to require central approval for all projects because of the resulting time delays and development of an excessive super-structure. Where referrals upstream are needed, the next higher level above the implementing agency should have the authority to approve or reject, but not to substitute projects.

71

Organisation and Operation

Technical Supervision

The standardisation and limitation of eligible project types plus the preparation of detailed project manuals will help reduce the need for technical supervision. Providing adequate transportation for engineering and supervisory staff will allow a programme to spread the available talent more widely, as will the conscious effort to train and use foremen. This is an area of frequent tension between the "quality" preferences of technical ministries and the need to execute many small projects simultaneously. The conflict can be reduced through continuing efforts to standardise and simplify both the projects and the technology.

Communication and Feedback

Once a public works programme has been established on sound policies, and an effective administrative system is built, it is not possible to leave it alone and expect that it will continue to operate satisfactorily. A successful programme will need constant supervision, adjustment to changing situations, and accommodation to lessons learned in its operation. Flexible administration, capable of making corrections in the programme during its operation, is as important as the initial design and the administrator must specifically design mechanisms for ensuring and facilitating communication. Communication from the field up to the administrator is the critical requirement; by comparison, downward communication in relatively easy. To ensure good upward communication, several steps are recommended. First, the programme administrator must do a great deal of field work himself. He must see how the programme is progressing at first hand and must talk to many people involved and affected by the programme. This should not be limited to programme officials but should include workers, villagers, and any others who have regular contact with the programme or are knowledgeable about it. Second, field administrators must be free to bring their views and problems to the administrator; he must have an "open door" policy and encourage communication between himself and the staff at all levels. The administrative system of such a programme cannot be hierarchical. Third, communication between levels should be officially sponsored and structured. In East Pakistan

there were semi-annual conferences of Works
Programme staff at the Academy for Rural Development. These conferences were always attended by the
Secretary for Local Government, who was responsible
for the Works Programme, and his deputies. They
gave field officers the opportunity through informal
conversations to express their views on all aspects
of programme administration, and provided top administrators the chance to discuss weaknesses and
problems or to present changes or new programme
directions. Fourth, the types of regular reporting
systems already suggested, that ensure the upward
flow of relevant financial and performance data, are
essential. The careful analysis of this data and
its use in adjusting programme procedures is basic.
Without mechanisms to encourage and facilitate the
flow of information and ideas, it will not be
possible to run an effective, innovative programme.

Records and Record-Keeping

Records in decentralised rural works programmes
must be the responsibility of all agencies involved
in the programme. Special efforts will have to be
made to structure and standardise record-keeping
procedure at the local level. Record keeping must
stress simplicity and clarity so that information
can be compiled and reported promptly and accurately. Individual project reports showing estimated and actual expenditures by category are
essential.

The basic data that must be kept and reported
include the following: total expenditures, expenditure by different types of projects, unit costs (ie
per kilometre of road), expenditures on labour and
on materials, total worker-days of employment
created (divided between skilled and unskilled).
Data on physical accomplishments are also needed.
This should be accumulated from reports of each
project carried out, giving size, general specifications, and labour and material inputs.

Each year the national level administrative
unit should aggregate this information and issue an
annual performance report. These reports will
permit comparisons of the relative efficacy of
labour-intensive with other construction techniques,
will serve as an overall indicator of programme
performance, and will suggest possible trouble spots
and desirable changes in programme performance.

Organisation and Operation

Scheduling Activities

A detailed and specific schedule or calendar is
very important in the operation of a rural works
programme, and assuring adherence to it is one of
the most important of the programme administrator's
responsibilities. Failure to coordinate effectively
on finances is one of the most frequently observed
weaknesses in public works programmes, resulting in
implementation delays and failure to achieve the
desired seasonal coordination. Such an operating
schedule should cover an entire year and should
specify the dates for such component activities as
project identification, approval, allocation of
funds, release of funds, interim and final
reporting, etc.

Worker-days of employment should be a basic
unit of accounting, available for each project. It
is disappointing to note the number of rural works
programmes for which no reliable figures are available on the amount of employment generated. The
programmes in Morocco and Tunisia, in contrast, use
the worker-day as the basic accounting unit in
project descriptions, allocations, and as a basis
for estimating material, capital and overhead costs.

Figure 1 suggests a sample yearly schedule for
a programme which has a limited work season. It
could be easily adapted to a year round schedule.
The figure is organised according to months of the
year and levels of agencies involved in implementation, starting with the Centre (National or
Regional), Intermediate (State, Province, District,
etc.), and Local (Village, County, etc.) and
suggests the functions, ie preparation of projects,
release of budget estimates, etc. that must be
included in the schedule, and the approximate times
needed to complete each of these functions.

Public Disclosure

Maximum use should be made of public
information and disclosure in order to develop
public interest and support for the programme and to
reduce the chance for financial corruption and
misappropriation. In East Pakistan in 1966, over
150,000 rural citizens served on local project
committees and were actively involved in the
selection, implementation and review process.
Simple procedures that have proven effective include
signs at each work site describing the project,

74

Figure 1.—Sample Yearly Work Schedule (assuming a 6-month work season)

Level of Action	Jan	Feb	Mar	April	May	June	July	Aug	Sep	Oct	Nov	Dec
Centre	Issue annual financial and performance report		Release half of work funds			Release half of work funds			Notify local units of estimated funds for next year			
	Final notice of funds available											
Intermediate											Technical review of action by project-approving authority	Annual evaluation and planning meeting
Local		Order materials. Final surveys. Estimates and preparation for work				Submit financial report		Plan and prepare projects for next year		Submit project proposals		
										Submit financial and performance reports		

<------------------------------Work Season------------------------------>

<------------------------------Audits and performance checks------------------------------>

giving the name of the implementing group, and spe-
cifying both the cost and the number of worker days
of employment that are to be provided. It is useful
to take photographs of each project at its start,
mid-way through and on completion. These photographs should be a permanent part of the individual
project record. At the completion of the project a
summary of costs, physical achievement, employment
created, purchases of non-labour inputs and the
names of the group and individuals responsible
should be available in printed form to anyone who is
interested. Public information and the pressures
that result from public interest are the most
effective means of ensuring that officials do not
misuse rural works programme funds.

Seasonality

Rural works programmes should be scheduled so
they operate during peak periods of unemployment.
There are two reasons for this. First, in most
countries rural unemployment is a seasonal phenomenon, related to crop planting, growing and
harvesting cycles. It is important that rural works
programmes be phased so as not to compete for labour
with agricultural activities during periods of peak
demand, thereby increasing the opportunity of
creating new jobs. The administrator will
frequently be subjected to pressures to prolong the
construction season, but is is essential that the
programme be limited in time so that it complements
and does not compete with the agricultural demand
for labour. Second, programmes that operate year-
round often attract a permanent set of workers who
are completely dependent on the programme for
employment; such a situation makes rural works a
welfare programme that is difficult to reduce and
whose workers acquire a relief mentality.

The Uses and Limits of Self-help

The concept of self-help is a practical and
laudable one. Self-help as a voluntary expression
of a community's desire for change and improvement
is one of the most powerful development instruments.
It mobilises new resources for development and
involves the people actively in their own affairs.
It is a primary technique for local initiative.
Such participation generally results in better use

of facilities created and the assurance that such
facilities will be maintained. Unfortunately the
self-help concept has frequently been used as a
means of exploitation of the lowest income groups in
rural works programmes. However, distinguishing
between genuine self-help and exploitation of low-
income labour is relatively easy.

Many rural works programmes use the self-help
principle to reduce the cost of the facilities
built. Such low-cost infrastructure programmes must
be examined very carefully. Self-help is not
employment creation. In many cases the term self-
help has been used to disguise forced labour. In
cases where labour is forced to contribute time,
labour efficiency is very low and in some cases even
directly counterproductive. In one case in
Ethiopia, workers receiving compensation at levels
substantially below the market wage rate were
directed to plant trees on the property of a large
landowner as part of a reforestation project.
Approximately half the trees were planted upside-
down, which for workers who make their living in
agricultural pursuits could not have been an
accident. There is a very simple test to determine
when self-help should be used. If the workers are
the primary beneficiaries of the projects in their
operational phase, then self-help or lower-than-
market wages are justified. If the workers are not
the primary beneficiaries, then a market wage should
be paid.

The Use of Food Commodities to Finance Rural Public Works

In the 1960s many rural public works programmes
were started because of the availability of food
commodities as a form of foreign assistance. The US
Food for Peace legislation (established by Public
Law 480 and widely known simply as "PL480") was
specifically designed to encourage the rural works
type of programme. In such programmes food commodities were normally used in two ways: (1) they were
sold and the proceeds were used to finance the
programmes, or (2) they were used as wage goods and
workers were paid in kind. More recently, the World
Food Programme has become an important supporter of
"food for work" programmes. The continued availability of foreign food resources for support of
rural works programmes poses a number of questions
for administrators. It is incontestable that

payment of wages in food commodities is awkward and adds to the administrative requirements of a programme. The problems of receiving, transporting, storing and distributing commodities, pricing, and of the acceptability of the commodities that are distributed, present serious issues with which the programme administrator must contend.

There are however some offsetting advantages: commodity wages reduce inflationary potential, reduce the extent of speculative food hoarding in periods of crisis and they help to ensure that wages are used to improve the nutritional intake of needy families. Most importantly, they represent a resource that must frequently be used in this form or foregone.

In considering these issues, ascertaining whether food can be sold to provide funds for the programme is a necessary starting point. This is clearly preferable to commodity wages and solves most of the problem of food aid but is not permitted under many aid programmes. If it is not possible, the positive and negative features must be weighed for the particular situation. The strongest case for commodity wage is in crisis situations where their anti-inflationary and anti-hoarding aspects are most helpful. To increase food availability in an area where normal crops have been destroyed or reduced is essential. The greatest problem of food wages in such situations is that there is not the time needed to schedule deliveries of commodities from abroad. However, in a number of countries this problem has been solved by borrowing from domestic food grain stocks and, over a longer period, replacing them with aid agency food commodities. Most food aid programmes are willing to make such arrangements.

The first stage in deciding whether food commodities are feasible depends on the size, dispersion and work season of the programme. Based on a standard calculation of three kilograms of grain per worker-day, it is possible to estimate the transport and storage capacity that will be needed. If it is assumed that commodity payments should be made within three kilometres of the work site, the requirements for local distribution and storage will be clear. In all cases, crisis and otherwise, an adequate state of infrastructure development is an important prerequisite for the use of food commodities. Since work will proceed on a schedule that will be determined by labour demand in agriculture and by rainy and dry seasons, it is essential that

food commodities can be moved and stored in such a
way as to ensure their availability at times when
work is progressing.

The administrator of a food for work programme
must consider carefully the ramifications of
managing such a programme. A week's wages in wheat
might weigh between ten and twenty kilograms.
Workers will need containers and will incur transportation costs if they have to transport these
"wages" very far. Such problems emphasise the
thought that must go into establishing an administrative system to handle commodity wages. The administrator must plan to have extra administrative
talent available to handle all the details of their
movement and storage. Specific scheduling of commodities becomes critical, and particular attention
must be given to their valuation so that workers'
real wages are comparable to market wages. It is
important to know if the commodities available are
acceptable to local tastes. There have been
instances where bulgar wheat or regular wheat was
distributed in rice-eating areas, or milk powder
where people are unfamiliar with it. In such cases,
the commodities are often sold by workers in the
local market for amounts much below their value.
This means that workers are receiving very low wages
and will probably be reluctant to work.

Finally, important nutritional questions must
go into a calculation of the quantities to be paid.
International comparisons suggest that a healthy
young man can move between 1.8 and 2.1 cubic metres
of earth a day. Nutritional studies in India and
Bangladesh suggest that an adult male engaged in
hard physical activity requires 3,000 to 3,500
Calories per day. Cereals, both wheat and rice,
provide about 350 Calories per 100g. As a result, a
worker needs roughly one kilogram of cereals per
day. However, it is obviously necessary to pay
workers more than just the food they consume, partly
to provide a work incentive and also to improve the
nutritional standards of the entire family. As a
result, two to three kilograms of foodgrain per
worker per day has become an international standard.
Some programmes have paid lower commodity wages to
women. Estimates from Bangladesh suggest that while
women can move only about two-thirds as much each
per day as male workers, their caloric requirements
when doing hard labour are close to those of men.
This is partly because many women of work age are
breast-feeding their children. Opportunity costs
for women workers may also be higher since many of

their work responsibilities such as child care, food
preparation or home maintenance, are not seasonal.
It is strongly recommended that a single food wage
be paid to male and female workers. [1]
On balance, the problems that accompany
commodity wages are substantial, and it is clearly
better to sell food aid commodities in the market to
provide funds for cash wages. However, commodity
wages may be justified if sale is not permitted, if
transportation and storage facilities are adequate,
and if the commodities available are acceptable to
the local people.

Maintenance

Maintaining works constructed by a rural works
programme is an important issue. Low-cost rural
works, such as dirt roads or unlined water channels,
need considerable recurring maintenance. Many of
these programmes' critics attack them on the basis
that this type of construction results in high continuing costs. However, given low initial costs,
rural works construction is generally lower cost
than alternative forms even with continuing maintenance costs, particularly if the cost stream over
time is discounted.

Despite the high need for maintenance on
typical rural works assets, several programmes have
specifically forbidden the use of programme funds
for this purpose, and only one made maintenance a
priority claim against continuing allocations. It
is the authors' view that maintenance is a normal
and appropriate expenditure for a rural works
programme, and that a system of required maintenance
of past projects as a limited first charge against
allocations, is highly desirable.

Most rural works programmes are more
interested in providing continuing seasonal
employment for unskilled workers than in creating a
very large employment programme in a short period
(Relief programmes are an exception). Maintenance
is generally very labour intensive and requires less
technical and supervisory effort than new projects.
Deferred maintenance of non-rural works projects
should be considered as appropriate for inclusion in
a rural works programme as new construction. In
Indonesia the first few years of the Kabupaten
programme were devoted to reconstructing the old
Javanese irrigation system that had deteriorated
over many years. Project designs should be

encouraged that permit incremental upgrading in subsequent years (eg improving road surfaces or lining irrigation channels) if use justifies the additional investment.

Many programmes have made maintenance the responsibility of the local community. While this arrangement has often resulted in under-maintained assets of low productivity, there are cases where at least some community contribution is appropriate. Some projects, primarily those that are directly productive, benefit a specific individual or group. An irrigation canal benefits those who draw irrigation water from it and it raises their incomes. In such cases taxing the beneficiaries for the full maintenance cost or, preferably, requiring them to maintain the facility, is appropriate. If maintenance is to be the responsibility of the local community, the programme administrator should ensure that the community has an adequate tax base and that local taxes are sufficiently progressive that taxing for maintenance purposes does not defeat the distributive objectives of the programme. For example, a head tax or a hut tax imposes a proportionately larger burden on the poor. To increase such taxes to support maintenance of a road would be to tax the poor disproportionately to maintain a facility that was of more benefit to the affluent.

Concluding Comments

This chapter has stressed specific steps that the administrator must take in implementing a programme. These steps will help an effective, flexible administrator with political backing to run a successful programme. The need for such a capable administrator must be emphasised. The manual is a management tool and cannot be a substitute for effective leadership. Any administrative system will have to be improved as experience is accumulated. This chapter has attempted to point out potential problem areas so that the administrator will be alerted; it has suggested ways in which problems can be reduced or eliminated. With these guidelines, the chances of a capable administrator running a successful rural works programme should be improved.

NOTES

1. For more information on this subject, see L C Chen "An Analysis of Per Capita Food Grain Availability in Bangladesh: a Systematic Approach to Food Planning", <u>The Bangladesh Development Review</u> Vol. III, No. 2, April 1975.

Chapter Six

MONITORING PROGRAMME PERFORMANCE

International experience with labour-intensive
rural public works programmes demonstrates that many
of them experience substantial changes over time.
In some cases these changes are intentionally
brought about by planners and administrators to
improve the functioning of the programme or to
respond to changing development priorities. Other
changes are unintentional and are frequently undesirable from the point of view of the programme administrator. On the other hand, some programmes continue relatively unchanged over long periods of time
and succeed in continuing to deliver substantial
benefits to their intended population target groups.
    This chapter discusses a number of specific
changes that have been observed in programmes over
time, and suggests indicators that may alert the
administrator to existing or potential problems.
Specific organisational, recording and accounting
systems must be organised to bring these changes to
the attention of the responsible implementing group
so that appropriate action can be taken to overcome
deviations that are considered undesirable. After
discussing a number of potentially important
changes, their indicators, and the sort of remedial
action that can be taken, the chapter concludes with
a discussion of a number of broad guidelines, based
on international experience, by which a particular
programme's performance may be judged.

Changes in the Types of Projects

    One of the clearest changes that can be antici-
pated over time is a shift in the profile of
projects toward those which are directly productive.
Table 6.1 summarises changes in four programmes for

which detailed project comparisons are possible over
at least a 5-year period. These are the programmes
in Bangladesh, Morocco, Pakistan, and Korea. Impressionistic evidence and comments from programme
administrators suggest that the same tendency has
been observed in a number of other programmes
elsewhere, including those in Tunisia and India. As
Table 6.1 shows, all four programmes experienced a
significant increase in the percentage of funds
spent on directly productive assets. No similar
generalisations can be made for economic infrastructure or social infrastructure expenditures, although
in only one case (Pakistan) did social infrastructure expenditures increase over time.

There are several probable reasons for this
increase in productive asset projects. Some of
these may be desirable from the programme planner's
point of view, and others may represent undesirable
trends and require investigation and remedial
action. Many rural works programmes start in emergency or crisis conditions. This was true of 7 out
of 19 programmes that existed in the 1960s and early
1970s. In several other cases, high levels of unemployment created an emergency atmosphere which gave
rise to initiation of a rural works programme. In
such conditions, economic infrastructure projects,
particularly the repair of existing roads and the
building of secondary and tertiary roads, is often
the easiest way to employ large numbers of people
quickly. The emphasis is on quick action and
planners are attracted to projects which can be
started immediately, are highly labour-intensive,
and require little engineering preparation.

Directly productive projects, such as irrigation schemes and land reclamation, generally require
more technical planning, longer lead times, and may
involve more participation by technical ministries
and larger numbers of skilled workers. It therefore
takes more time to identify, engineer, coordinate
and implement these projects. In the Scarcity
Relief programmes begun in India in the early 1970s,
for example, directly productive projects began to
replace road building activities such as earth-
moving and the breaking of rocks. As the programme
continued, time was available to coordinate with
planning agencies and to implement projects that
were already scheduled for inclusion in future
development programmes.

Another reason for the shift in composition of
projects is the need to justify continuing appro-
priation on the basis of economic efficiency. As

Table 6.1.--Relative Priority Accorded to Different
Types of Rural Works Projects over Time

| Country | Period | Type of project | | |
| | | Directly productive | Infrastructure | |
			Economic	Social
		(in per cent of total funds)		
Bangladesh	1963-64	6.7	72.2	21.1
	1967-68	15.5	71.5	13.0
Percentage change		+131	-1	-40
Morocco	1961-62	35.6	46.3	18
	1971-72	46.3	34.6	19
Percentage change		+30	-26	+5
Pakistan	1963-64	11.5	21.2	67.3
	1968-69	14.9	36.0	49.1
Percentage change		+29	+70	-28
South Korea				
NCS	1961-62	46	48	6
Self-help	1968	61	24	15
Percentage change		+33	-50	+150

Chapter Three suggested, it is easier to show
specific benefits, both in terms of long-term
employment creation and in terms of conventional
benefit-cost analysis, for directly productive than
for other classes of projects. The LCSD programme
in Tunisia was started as a pure relief operation in
1960, but when the Planning Department was formed
three years later the programme was shifted to that
department and the accent on economic productivity

was greatly increased both in project content and in the publicity given to the programme. Similarly, the Relief Workers Programme in Mauritius in the 1960s stressed the provision of employment and the improvement of urban life through expenditures on social amenities. Over the years and with changes in programme name, the focus has shifted to a rural development basis, stressing such highly productive projects as bench terracing.

From the programme planner's viewpoint, this trend of relief programmes to shift toward economically productive projects is often desirable but it may be overdone, depending on programme priorities. If providing for improved rural education and health care are primary programme aims, an excessive shift to directly productive projects would be undesirable. A shift to directly productive assets may also indicate a shift in the distributive nature of the programme, as more and more operating phase benefits are diverted from target to non-target groups. The possibility of such a reduction of benefits is greater if the pattern of land holdings is extremely unequal and if important land holders are able to dominate the project selection process through participatory or bureaucratic pressures. A study in Pakistan in the 1960s showed a clear negative correlation between the concentration of land holdings in village areas and the proportion of rural works expenditure that was devoted to social infrastructure projects. [1]

Shifts in Programme Benefits

A related change that can affect the distributive nature of the programme and is more difficult to verify and control is a change in the location of projects in order to divert benefits from target to wealthier land holding groups. District officials in Maharashtra reported that they kept project siting decisions out of the hands of the local panchayat councils for fear that both project type and location would be dominated by the larger landlords. Despite such precautions, an investigating team studying relief efforts in Maharashtra reported that the siting of percolation tanks favoured the large landholders on a systematic basis. The investigators reported cases of active opposition by landlords when project location would provide benefits to small farmers. [2] The DNOCS programme in Northeast Brazil during the 1950s was a clear example of diversion of benefits by improper influences on both project type and project selection. Although drought relief was the declared objective, projects were chosen by large landowners or officials who represented their own interests. One result was irrigation systems located on private lands. Roads were built through areas occupied by very large "estates". In sum, few benefits accrued to the poor, who were the nominal population target group.

Possible steps to minimise programme distortion by changes in project siting include regular reporting and analysis of project decisions, inclusion in project descriptions of the landholding pattern in the areas that will be benefited, fees or user charges where directly productive projects clearly benefit farmers whose landholdings exceed some minimum level, and adequate staff to investigate promptly allegations that undue influences are affecting project location decisions.

Pressures to Reduce Labour Intensity

Influences that will attempt to reduce the degree of labour intensity can be expected in many rural works programmes. This is a particularly destructive form of programme alteration, since a high degree of unskilled labour-intensity in the construction phase of projects is the greatest single source of target group benefits. Pressure for greater capital intensity may come from several sources. Technical ministries that are involved in project implementation may have continuing restrictions about the use of labour-intensive technologies and may try to revert to the capital-intensive techniques with which they are more familiar. A shift in project composition to more sophisticated and technically complex projects may result in higher material, capital, and skilled labour costs, with a reduction in target group benefits. For example, the inclusion of hard surfacing and more culverts will raise the material and skilled labour cost of a road, as will replacing earth with cement in retaining walls or water channels in reclamation, drainage and irrigation projects. In some programmes the use of contractors has been associated with decreased labour intensity. These potential influences are strengthened by the fact that the unskilled workers, who are the nominal target group, are generally unorganised, politically

weak, frequently illiterate, and in a poor position
to defend their interests.

Some of the information about pressures to
decrease labour intensity is impressionistic since
detailed time series data on categories of costs is
not generally available. No existing rural work-
programme has experienced an increase of labour-
intensity over time. Of the four programmes for
which figures are available for eight years or more,
as shown in Table 6.2, two showed clearly declining
trends, one showed a sharp drop in the last three
years, and one was relatively stable.

What steps can a programme planner take to
assure continued labour intensity? The one country
whose figures show a sustained high level of labour
intensity, Morocco, is the only one of the four
which uses man-days of labour as a basic accounting
unit for allocations and reporting. Incomplete
figures for Tunisia, which also reports in man-day
terms, suggest that labour intensity has remained
high. In the Pakistan and Bangladesh programmes,
where labour intensity in the most recently reported
year was estimated to be less than 20 per cent,
worker-days of employment were not the central unit
of reporting, and frequently had to be estimated
from fragmentary information. In addition to the
consistent collection of data on employment generation, programme guidelines can limit permissible
overheads and material expenses to fixed proportions
of unskilled labour costs, and specify through
project manuals the technology that is to be
followed. In these ways, it should be possible to
keep factor proportions in line with programme
goals.

Changes in Levels of Administrative Responsibility

Another set of indicators that can suggest
possible danger signs for a rural works programme,
including the question of preserving labour
intensity, has to do with changes in the nature and
level of the project implementing agency. Local-
elected officials generally spread employment as
broadly as possible, using a maximum of unskilled
labour. Contractors, who have been used to
implement projects in about half of the existing
programmes, generally preferred more capital-
intensive methods than local officials. This may be
a result of a desire to use capital equipment
already owned, or of the same price distortions,

Table 6.2.--Labour Intensity over Time [a]

Bangladesh[b]		Morocco[c]		Pakistan[d]		South Korea[e]	
Per cent	Period	Per cent	Period	Per cent	Period	Per cent	Period
68	1962-63	80	1961	29	1963-64	94	1964
60	1963-64	80	1962	31	1964-65	91	1965
59	1964-65	79	1963	30	1965-66	89	1966
54	1965-66	94	1964	29	1970-72	85	1967
54	1966-67	97	1965			88	1968
27	1969	90	1966			82	1969
16	1973	86	1967			82	1969
		94	1968			79	1971
		90	1969			70	1971
		90	1969			70	1972
		87	1970				
		84	1971				

a   Figures in the per cent columns are labour costs as a
percentage of total programme expenses.

b   Figures for Bangladesh for 1962-63 through 1966-67 are
adapted from John W. Thomas, "The Rural Works Program and
East Pakistan Development", unpublished PhD thesis, Harvard
University (1968). Figures for 1969 and 1973 are based on
small sample surveys conducted by Thomas.

c   Figures for Morocco are from annual reports of Promotion
Nationale adjusted for some estimated excluded costs. The
percentages are believed to be overstated, but on a
consistent basis.

d   Figures for Pakistan for 1963-64 to 1965-66 are adapted from
figures in John W. Thomas, "The Rural Public Works Program
in East Pakistan", in G. F. Papanek and W. P. Falcon,
Development Policy II: The Pakistan Experience, Harvard
University Press (1971). Figures for 1970-72 are adapted
from data provided by the Departments of Local Government in
the Provinces of Punjab, Frontier and Sind.

e   Figures for South Korea are adapted from data provided by
the Korean Development Institute. The decline in the last
two years shown reflects the conversion of the programme
from land reclamation to more capital-intensive paved roads.
Labour intensity is believed to be overstated, but on a
consistent basis.

favouring the substitution of capital for labour, that aggravated unemployment in the first place. The use of contractors also makes it more difficult to collect uniform, detailed and dependable information on programme costs and the amount of employment generated. A programme administrator can anticipate that a change in the project implementing agency will affect labour intensity and a move away. from implementation by locally elected officials suggests the possibility of decreased use of unskilled labour.

Changes in the administrative level at which projects are selected and implemented can also be an indication of important changes in programme impact. In West Pakistan, programme guidelines called for 70 per cent of programme funds to be distributed through local council projects. However, this percentage was achieved only in the first year, 1963-64. Two years later the local council share had declined to 36 per cent, with more and more project decisions taken at the district and divisional levels. Citizen project committees became less important, and contractors rapidly took over implementation of over 75 per cent of the projects. The programme became less responsive to local needs and failed almost totally to achieve its announced goal of invigorating local government and leadership, and mobilising the rural population for development purposes. In contrast, during the early years of the East Pakistan programme, implementation of projects shifted downstream from district to thana county levels, the use of contractors was reduced and subsequently eliminated, and the programme grew increasingly responsive to local needs and local initiative.

In order to preserve labour intensity and to help achieve local mobilisation aims, if such exist, programme administrators should investigate thoroughly the causes and implications of any tendency to move the responsibility for implementation to higher administrative levels.

Politicisation of Programmes

A final area in which changes--generally destructive--have been observed in rural works programmes is an increase in the degree of programme politicisation. Chapter Three pointed out the problems of politicisation in participatory programmes but there are many other ways this takes

place. It is important to recognise that unemployment and poverty are political as well as economic
problems and that rural works programmes have political as well as economic aims. Table 6.3 summarises the non-economic circumstances in which
thirteen public works programmes were started and
also suggests the role played by foreign advisors or
foreign aid agencies in their beginnings. While it
is difficult to establish causal links, it is
instructive to note the number of cases in which an
approaching election or a threat to law and order
has accompanied the decision to start a works
programme.

The hope of political gain is a reasonable
expectation in starting a rural works programme.
The delivery of benefits to low income portions of
the rural population, often missed by other types of
development programmes, can properly lead to
significantly increased support for a regime.
Problems arise and programmes are weakened when
excessive politicisation replaces performance
criteria with criteria of political loyalty, opening
the door for a variety of abuses, including substantial financial corruption.

The history of the East Pakistan/Bangladesh,
the Pakistan, and the Morocco programmes demonstrates many of the problems attendant on excessive
politicisation and suggests ways in which programme
administrators might attempt to control the effects
of political influences.

Bangladesh. East Pakistan's Works Programme
was started in 1962 without powerful government
sponsorship. A pilot programme conducted indepen-
dently by the Academy of Rural Development in
Comilla was already demonstrating that local
councils could successfully implement a seasonal
decentralised labour-intensive public works
programme. The Basic Democracies system, created in
1959, was intended to strengthen local councils in
order to provide effective government and promote
local development. A history of active local
government plus relatively egalitarian land holding
patterns provided the basis for broad participation
in these councils. The Secretary of Basic
Democracies saw the Comilla programme as a potential
development vehicle for the local councils.
Following a period of opposition by the Finance
Minister at the centre, the programme was commenced,
partly as a result of emergency conditions following
monsoon floods. Presidential endorsement of the
programme was withheld for another year.

Table 6.3.--Conditions Associated with the Adoption of Works Programmes

Country	Year	Programme	Political events	Foreign advisers or foreign aid
Afghanistan	1971	Provincial Development Programme	New government. Capable, powerful minister assigned to food crisis.	Bilateral agency assisted formation. Food aid available.
Bangladesh	1962	Works Programme	Prior pilot project; active provincial political support to bolster Basic Democracies system	Adviser-recommended. Food aid agreement signed.
Brazil	1909	Departmento Nacional da Obras Contra as Sëcas (DNOCS)	Activist northeasterner responsible for public works and transportation.	None
India	1971	Crash scheme for Rural Employment	Naxalite disturbances.	None
	1970	Drought Prone Areas Programme	Anti-poverty campaign for approaching elections.	None
Indonesia	1970	Kabupaten Programme	First political party formed and elections promised; effort to form new constituency base at district level.	Adviser-recommended and planned
Jamaica	1972	Impact Works Programme	New government elected with clear employment mandate.	None

Table 6.3, continued

Country	Year	Programme	Political events	Foreign advisers or foreign aid
Mauritius	1972	Travail pour Tous	Dock strike; threat of sugar estate strike; growing political opposition—government lost sensitive by-elections.	None
Morocco	1961	Promotion Nationale	None	Bilateral agency support; food aid
Pakistan	1963	Rural Works Programme	Desire to build constituency base through Basic Democracies system; approaching presidential elections.	Adviser-recommended. Food aid available.
South Korea	1961	National Construction Service	New government; activist students mobilised.	Active bilateral agency support; food aid available.
Trinidad-Tobago	1970	Special Works Programme	Civil disturbances by army and youth reflecting unemployment.	None
Tunisia	1959	Lutte Contra le Sous Developpement	Removal of French support and skilled expatriates.	Bilateral agency support; food aid available.

In its first few years, the programme operated quite effectively. Public participation was active, with democratic checks on the performance of public officials. Project quality was high, with over 55 per cent of programme funds spent on wages. In the election of 1965, the government won an unexpected victory in East Pakistan, which was widely attributed to the success of the Works Programme. From this point on, politicians placed increasing pressure on the programme to shift the allocation of funds to reflect political loyalties to President Ayub and his party. The programme rapidly deteriorated as political purposes replaced economic aims. By 1973, the proportion of programme funds represented by wages was reduced to 16 per cent. Implementation by contractors--predominantly supporters of the regime--had replaced implementation by the local councils. Overstatement of project expenditures and direct misuse of funds were common. Some of these changes are summarised in Table 6.4, which shows the clear deterioration of the programme between 1967 and 1973. It was apparent that the principal beneficiaries of the programme were no longer the rural poor, but contractors, large farmers and traders--the groups from which the Basic Democracies were drawn. Rural frustration over the abuse of power by the Basic Democrats, including misuse of programme funds, was indicated by the many acts of violence against them in the early months of 1969.

West Pakistan. West Pakistan's Rural Works Programme started in 1963 with clear support from the military regime. Unlike East Pakistan, there was no history of broad political activism, and the distribution of land, income and political power was far more concentrated. By following the East Pakistan model, using local councils as the implementing agencies for the programme, the regime intended to help the rural middle class solidify the political power they had gained from the 1959 land reform and from the introduction of the Basic Democracies system.

A major stated objective of the programme was the creation of employment for poor and unskilled rural workers through labour-intensive projects. The consistent failure of the programme to fulfill this objective supports the view that none of the domestic interest groups responsible for introducing and supporting it (the national regime, the bureaucracy, and the middle and large farmers) were committed to the objective of employment creation.

Table 6.4.--Changes in the Bangladesh Works
           Programme Between 1967 and 1973

Year	Works programme as a % of development expenditure	Wage payments as a % of total expenditure	Per cent of projects implemented by contractors	Type of projects receiving largest share of funds
1964	13.3	60	--	Dirt roads
1967	6.7	62	8	Dirt roads
1969	5.7	27	--	Bridges and culverts
1973	3.2	16	94	Paved roads

SOURCE: Figures for Bangladesh for 1962-63 through
        1966-67 are adapted from John W. Thomas,
        The Rural Works Program and East Pakistan
        Development, unpublished PhD thesis,
        Harvard University (1968). Figures for
        1969 and 1973 are based on small sample
        surveys conducted by Thomas.
NOTE: Use of (--) indicates data are not
        available.

From 1963 to 1972 an average of only 30 per cent of
total programme costs was spent on wages and over 40
per cent of the wage bill was for skilled labour--
the highest proportion of any of the programmes
implemented in the 1960s. The changes that took
place over time merely represented the consolidation
of control by dominant interest groups. By 1964 the
large landlords, who had been distrustful at first
of the Basic Democracies system, made clear their
desire to cooperate with the military regime. By
the elections of 1965 they were once again in
control of the local councils and had re-established
their previous partnership with the Civil Service of
Pakistan, extending to joint domination of the works
programme.
    The Rural Works Programme also had the osten-
sible objectives of activating broadly representa-

tive government, and mobilising rural workers in
support of general development aims. However, the
realities of income and power concentration and the
domination of the programme by the elite bureaucracy
and the landlords meant that those goals had little
chance of being realised. An earlier section
mentioned the decline in local council implementation and the domination of the implementation
process by contractors. In 1972 the programme,
renamed the People's Work Programme, was redesigned
to alter its shortcomings, and to meet the new
government's commitment to improve conditions of the
rural poor. Its basic purposes of substantial
employment creation, construction of useful assets
in response to locally defined needs, and the mobilisation of the people through development of local
initiative and leadership, were reaffirmed. Yet,
despite the national government's objectives, the
absence of functioning local government, the lack of
central control, and the politicisation of the
programme in the provinces, caused the programme to
become a vehicle for local patronage and the enrich-
ment of private interests, some officials, contractors and politicians. [3]

   Morocco. Promotion Nationale in Morocco has
operated consistently since 1961 with reasonably
high labour intensity and economic efficiency, and a
generally stable profile of projects. It was
founded by royal decree, and the King's continuing
active interest in the programme helps contribute to
its stability. The labour-intensive approach was
built into the programme from the beginning by
making worker days of labour the basic unit of
reporting, scheduling and auditing, and for the
release of food supplied for wages. A high proportion of programme funds are disbursed through
regional governments which control the programme
with advice from technical ministries. Promotion
Nationale provides important political benefits to
the regional administration at all levels, from the
Regional Governor to the local sheikh, and offers
the regional governments their largest single source
of welfare payments and unemployment relief. Since
it is generally popular with its target groups, it
is an important source of support for the regime.
The technical ministries receive about 15 per cent
of programme funds. While there have been some
complaints within the Ministry of Agriculture and
Public Works that unskilled labour and poor disci-
pline result in unacceptably low productivity and
reduced standards, and the "welfare" function of the

programme conflicts with the Ministry's "technical" role, the labour intensity of the programme has not been affected. The technical ministries often find the programme useful since they can select their own projects and thus supplement their regular activities.

The programme was never intended to alter basic economic or political relationships, but was conceived as a solution to a visible and recurrent form of crisis. Since it does not seek to change the basic distribution of scarce resources, intermediate groups such as landlords and wealthy farmers do not feel threatened by it. It was implemented through existing administrative structures, provided new forms of patronage in a system that was basically non-competitive, and produced increased support for the regime from existing clienteles. The programme is not ideologically charged and makes no attempt to involve target groups in innovative organisations.

Several conclusions follow from these three examples, and from a number of other programmes studied, which may enable programme administrators to avoid the worst effects of programme politicisation:

1.   Success in the programme's reaching stated objectives will be influenced by the reality of interest group structure, the sensitivity of the regime to group interests and the nature of the surrounding social and political environment. It follows that a rural works programme should be designed to operate in a specific set of political and social conditions with the expectation that dynamic changes will continue to influence programme performance.

2.   A programme is more likely to encounter strong political pressures if it is highly redistributive, employs decentralised decision making with widespread participation of intermediate groups in the decision process and if it operates in an environment where the distribution of political and economic power and assets, particularly land, is highly skewed.

3.   The most critical factor in avoiding destructive politicisation is the political will and/or capacity at the centre to resist strong regional or local pressures. A national coordinating committee may be helpful in emphasising the economic advantages of the programme, thereby ensuring high level political support and reducing the risk of disruptive inter-bureaucratic political

rivalries. In every programme it is necessary to
share benefits with non-target groups. This is a
political cost if the programme is to function at
all. However, if the national regime comes to see
the programme principally in political terms, there
is a high probability that rural works programmes
will see their original purposes eroded and new
beneficiaries created.

Paradoxically, the history of the East Pakistan
programme suggests that the enforcement of
performance standards may yield substantial support
for a regime, while attempts to manipulate the
programme for political purposes may engender
popular antagonism. Over the long run, the
political benefits accruing to a regime may be
inversely correlated with its attempts to manipulate
a programme for political support.
As the preceding sections have made clear,
rural works programmes are constantly subject to
pressures for change in many dimensions. While
programme administrators must necessarily be
flexible and innovative, they must also recognise
these pressures and resist those that would under-
mine the basic objectives of the programme. Within
the limitations suggested above, the procedures
suggested in Chapter Five for organising programmes,
ensuring good information flow and the continuing
analysis of information will be essential to
effective administration of the programme.
Knowledge of precisely what is happening will enable
the administrator continually to enforce the established programme procedures and, with political
support, use his position to ensure that programme
activities and performance remain directed toward
achieving the programme's basic goals.

International Guidelines

Varied experiences with rural works programmes
in a large number of countries provide the basis for
a number of guidelines by which the performance of
any particular programme may better be judged.
These guidelines are necessarily general, and their
applicability will differ considerably from
programme to programme depending on the specific
context and mix of purposes. There are also
problems of data reliability and comparability.
With these warnings in mind, there are still a
number of general guidelines and relationships that
may help programme planners in an ex ante sense to

think realistically about the potential and the limitations of programmes they may be considering. In an ex post sense, the guidelines can help the programme planner identify weaknesses in an existing programme and devise ways in which performance can be improved and strengthened.

Many of these guidelines have already been suggested in earlier sections but for easy reference they are summarised here as well:

1.   Employment creation. Standards were suggested in Chapter Four for the total proportion of programme funds that should be devoted to wages. If this proportion drops below 40 per cent, serious questions must be asked about the programme. In addition, approximate labour intensities for projects in each of the three broad categories were also suggested. Finally, the issue of long term--or operating phase--employment was discussed and the rough ratio of 5 or 6 to 1 for construction phase employment to operating phase employment was suggested.

2.   Wage rates. Wage rates vary widely among programmes but in those cases where they are substantially below market levels, the productivity of labour drops noticeably. If a programme is not to become a programme of transfer payments to low income groups, it is important to ensure reasonable wage rates.

3.   Economic returns. Rural works programmes can produce attractive economic returns. If they do not do so, careful analysis of the programmes should be undertaken to determine the underlying causes of inefficiency.

4.   Cost of employment creation. Table 6.5 shows the costs of creating a worker-day of construction employment based on wage rates paid in the early 1970s. There are great variations between countries. Where costs are below $0.75 per worker-day, it must be assumed workers are being paid wages substantially below market wages. When costs exceed $1.25, it is necessary to look for inefficiency in the programme. (The exception is Colombia, where the programme was designed to build higher quality roads, but still at a cost below capital-intensive methods).

5.   Programme size. It is difficult to make useful international comparisons on the question of programme size. The scale of a programme must be determined by need and the capacity to support rural works in each country. Table 6.5 shows the absolute costs of various programmes and, as a proxy for

Monitoring Programme Performance

Table 6.5.--International Comparison of Programme
            Characteristics

Country	Cost of creating one worker-day of employment (US$)	Average annual programme cost (million US$)	Expenditure as a per cent of of fixed capital formation	Foreign aid as a per cent of total pro-gramme costs
Afghanistan	0.98	5.4	6.5a	77
Bangladesh	0.97	27.8	8.0b	45
NE Brazil	0.58	36.3	3.6c	0
Columbia	3.87	3.8	0.25	47
Ethiopia Tigre Province	0.32	0.14	0.05	14
India Crash Scheme	0.50	89.4	0.95	0
Drought Prone Areas	0.67	25.5	0.29	0
Indonesia Kabupaten	0.71	26.8	1.3	0
Jamaica	9.51	22.9	6.4	0
South Korea	0.57	15.3	1.4	63
Mauritius	1.85	2.5	8.7d	52
Morocco	0.88	15.4	4.4	26
Pakistan	3.17	13.8	3.4b	60
Tunisia	0.75	23.8	10.7	19

a   The figure is the percentage of total government expenditure.

b   The figure is the percentage of development expenditure.

c   The figure is the percentage for the region only.

d   The figure is the percentage of public sector capital
    formation.

relative size, the expenditure on rural works as a percentage of fixed capital formation. Figures given in Chapter Four on the amount of employment created in relation to agricultural labour force provide another perspective on relative programme size.

6. Sources of financing. Table 6.5 shows the percentages of foreign financing in various programmes. Over half the existing programmes have been supported by foreign aid and, in many of these cases, aid has met more than half the costs. The implications of this have been pointed out: a pressure toward administrative centralisation, the need to comply with donor requirements, the need sometimes to use food as wages and, where foreign aid represents a substantial percentage of the total, a dependence on foreign decisions to maintain the programme.

Conclusion

This chapter has attempted to provide the rural works administrator with practical guidelines for monitoring the progress of a programme. The administrator's task is particularly difficult since there are no clearly established patterns to determine how a new style programme such as rural works will operate. Furthermore, these programmes are constantly changing and under pressure for changes that would alter performance and reduce the prospects of achieving the fundamental purpose of the programmes. This chapter has shown what some of these pressures are likely to be, how they will affect programme performance, and how to provide indicators that will alert the administrator to their existence. With this knowledge of the pressures on the programme, the administrator will be better able to evaluate actions that are required to prevent adverse effects by responding to change appropriately.

NOTES

1. Burki, S. J. "Interest Group Involvement in West Pakistan Rural Works Program" Public Policy, Vol. XIX, No. 1, 1971.
2. Godbole, Achyug. "Productive Relief Works for the Rich", Economic and Political Weekly,

Bombay, 28 April 1973, p. 773.
    3.   A frank and critical review is provided by
the Evaluation of the People's Works Program,
Planning and Development Division, Government of
Pakistan, August, 1975.

Chapter Seven

CONCLUSION

      This manual is intended to assist developing
nations in using rural works programmes as a tool
for dealing with rural unemployment and poverty. It
is based on an analysis of twenty-four past or
existing programmes and provides a summary of that
experience in ways that should apply to both new and
continuing programmes. <u>It takes the position that</u>
<u>rural works programmes are very useful instruments</u>
<u>of development policy.</u> <u>They can promote several</u>
<u>objectives simultaneously and must be considered by</u>
<u>any country seriously concerned about rural unem-</u>
<u>ployment and poverty.</u> <u>However, rural works are</u>
<u>not appropriate for all such situations.</u> Therefore
the manual discusses the potential strengths and
limitations of rural works programmes, analysing the
issues that are generally raised when a programme is
being considered.
      For the country which decides on the basis of
this discussion that a rural works programme would
contribute to the solution of its problems, the
manual has set forth the issues that should be
considered when designing such a programme and has
suggested organisational procedures for achieving
the best possible results. Based on the experience
of other countries which have undertaken rural works
programmes, guidelines for the continuing monitoring
and administration of a programme have been
suggested. This has been done with the expectation
that some countries will be encouraged to attempt
rural works programmes and others will understand
why such programmes will not effectively address
their unemployment problems. For those that do
attempt programmes, this manual should improve their
chances for success appreciably.
      However, the role of the manual must also be
seen in perspective. There is no magic formula for

rural works, and strict adherence to the suggestions
in this manual will not necessarily ensure success.
It is therefore important to make clear some of the
factors that are outside the purview of this manual
but which are nevertheless crucial to the results of
a programme.

    1.   <u>Political commitment to programme goals.</u>
The goals of employment, development and the relief
of rural poverty are articulated by many countries,
but effective action in dealing with them requires a
much deeper political commitment. Poverty, unemployment and underdevelopment exist in part because
the economic system has served some groups more
effectively than others. To alter this situation is
to make new commitments to previously neglected
groups, redressing an existing imbalance. This will
inevitably incur opposition and pressures, both
overt and subtle, to restore the prior system or to
alter rural works to benefit groups other than those
with low incomes. Even with skillful management and
success in ensuring that some benefits accrue to the
groups most likely to oppose rural works, opposition
will emerge. Unless there is a strong political
commitment to adhere to the basic objectives of the
programme and to reinforce the procedures that serve
these objectives, the programme will, over time,
undergo a fundamental alteration which will change
its political purposes. To understand these political pressures, it is necessary to have some perspective on rural works in relation to policies dealing
with rural poverty. Rural works must be classified
as moderate reform programmes. They rarely redis-
tribute resources in sufficient magnitude to alter
relative positions on the income scale, in the way a
basic land reform does. On the other hand, since
they are designed to yield benefits to low-income
groups, they do not reinforce the status quo. When
seen in this context, the political attractiveness
of rural works is clear; the fact that they will
arouse opposition at some point is also clear.

    2.   <u>High calibre leadership.</u> The director of
an effective rural works programme will have to be
an administrator of very considerable talent. The
administrative requirements of such a programme are
far greater than in most development programmes.
Contrary to the case with more familiar programmes,
a decentralised programme of this type is a relatively new phenomenon in developing nations and will
require great capacity to analyse programme progress
and to learn from experience. This takes a highly
flexible administrative style and great perception

on the part of programme leadership. The pressures
cited mean that the programme's leadership will have
to be determined to resist strong pressures for
alteration in the programme. The administrator will
have to be non-hierarchical in behaviour and willing
and able to deal with personnel involved with the
programme at all levels. He (or she) will have to
encourage subordinates to communicate frankly about
the strengths and weaknesses of the programme and
then be willing to act on these views when they are
valid. In addition, the administrator will have to
emphasise the development of the capacity of people
at all levels of programme administration. Training
on a regular basis, particularly at the lower levels
of implementation, is essential. Rural works should
be seen as a skill development programme for both
workers and local administrative personnel and not
just a job creation programme. This emphasis on
people is particularly important in an innovative
programme of this sort where the people involved
will have to be committed to the objectives of the
programme and must be willing to make an extra
effort to have it succeed.

　　　3.　Supporting programmes and policies. This
manual has emphasised the point that rural works
programmes are not a solution to unemployment or
poverty. They must be used in conjunction with
other programmes and must be supported by other
policies. Too often there have been unrealistic
expectations for rural works. Many countries have
assumed, mistakenly, that if a works programme is
started there is no need for other efforts to
correct unemployment and poverty. Such an attitude
has generally resulted in limited success in
reaching intended goals and a tendency to dismiss
rural works as superficial and unsuccessful.
Attention must be given to other policies that
affect these objectives, and additional programmes
must be undertaken that will reach other members of
the population target groups, such as the very young
or the very old or the sick. If these supporting
efforts are made, there is reason to expect a rural
works programme to operate successfully. Frequently
rural works have been independent programmes without
formal association with other programmes aimed at
the same objectives. More consideration should be
given to having rural works as part of a comprehensive rural development effort.

　　　If these conditions are satisfied, the
prospects of a successful rural works programme are
good. In the next steps of programme design and

implementation this manual becomes particularly important as a management tool. It should serve both as a design manual in establishing a programme and as a reference work during the period of implementation.

All development programmes encounter difficulties. To overlook the types of problems that experience teaches us may arise during implementation would be to diminish the possibility of a successful programme. This manual has therefore stressed likely areas of difficulty and has suggested means of avoiding or minimising them. This accent on potential problems and on the high demands such innovative programmes place on a nation's administrative and implementing capabilities must be seen within a basically positive framework. It is the authors' view that rural works programmes are a desirable policy option for many developing countries, and that they present an unusual opportunity to make realistic progress against basic problems of employment, poverty and unequal income distribution. They also present an opportunity to improve the extent and calibre of local planning, to increase the degree of grass roots involvement in the development process, and to build institutionalised capacities for participation in that process.

APPENDIX

BIBLIOGRAPHY AND SUPPLEMENTARY REFERENCE MATERIAL

This appendix incorporates the references cited in the manual and includes additional material which would be of value to those considering rural works programmes or involved in planning or administering programmes. Depending upon their nature, references are grouped under six different headings

I. GENERAL REFERENCES

Bhaduri, A. and M. A. Rahman (eds.). Studies in Rural Participation. (Oxford and IBH Publishing Co., New Delhi, 1982)
Checci and Co. Food for Peace: An Evaluation of PL480 Title II, Washington D.C. vol. K, 1972
Harris, John R. and Michael P. Todaro. 'Migration, Unemployment and Development: A Two-Sector Analysis,' American Economic Review, vol. LX, no. 1, (1970), pp.126-42
Thomas, John W, Shahid Javed Burki, David G. Davies, Richard M. Hook. Employment and Development. Report to the World Bank, mimeographed, April 1975
World Bank. International Migration in LDC's: A Survey of the Literature, (World Bank Staff Working Paper, Washington, 1975)

II. EMERGENCY EMPLOYMENT SCHEMES AND SPECIAL EMPLOYMENT PROGRAMMES

Arlès, J. P. 'Emergency Employment Schemes', International Labour Review, vol. 109, no. 1, (1974)
Gaude, J., N. Phan-Thuy and C. van Kempen. 'Evaluation of Special Public Works Programmes', International Labour Review, vol. 123, no. 2

107

(1984)

Gaude, J. and N. Phan-Thuy. Flows of Benefits Analysis of Special Public Works Programmes: A Methodological Approach. (International Labour Office, World Employment Programme Working Paper 2-24/18, Geneva, 1982)

Guha, S. 'Income Redistribution through Labour-Intensive Public Rural Works', International Labour Review, vol. 120, no. 1 (1981)

World Bank. Public Works Programmes in Developing Countries: A Comparative Analysis, (World Bank Staff Working Paper No. 224, Washington, 1975)
_____. World Bank Staff Working Paper No. 172, 1974.

III. TECHNICAL GUIDELINES AND MANUALS

Costa, E. et al. Guidelines on the Organisation of Special Labour-Intensive Works Programmes. (International Labour Office, Geneva, 1980)

Garnier, Ph. Introduction to Special Public Works Programmes. (International Labour Office/United Nations Development Programme, Geneva, 1982)

Guérin, L. Report on Tools, Equipment and Local Materials for Special Labour-intensive Public Works Schemes in India, the Philippines, Tanzania (International Labour Office, Geneva, 1980)

Guha, S. Popular and Target Group Participation in Special Public Works Programmes: Conceptual Dimensions, Relevant Policies and Some Practical Guidelines. (International Labour Office, Geneva, 1982)

Knowles, M. Manual on Low-cost Building Construction. (International Labour Office, Geneva, 1981)

Leblond, B. and L. Guérin. Soil Conservation: Project Design and Implementation Using Labour-Intensive Techniques. (International Labour Office/United Nations Development Programme, Geneva, 1983)

IV TRAINING DOCUMENTS AND MATERIALS

Financial Control for Special Public Works Programmes. ILO/UNDP Training Programme (136 pages). (International Labour Office, Geneva, 1985)

Bibliography and Supplementary Reference Material

ILO/UNDP Training Course I. Planning and Evaluation of Special Public Works Programmes. A set of
15 booklets (600 pages) covering basic concepts,
the economic planning context, criteria for
applicability, programme design and socio-economic
evaluation. (International Labour Office, Geneva,
n.d.)
ILO/UNDP Training Course II. Organisation, Institution Building, Financing, Worker Training and
Working Conditions. A set of 10 booklets (400
pages) covering institutional framework and
staffing, target group participation and socio-
political aspects, budgeting and resource
mobilisation, education and training of workers,
nature of working conditions and standard
regulations. (International Labour Office,
Geneva, n.d.)
ILO/UNDP Training Course III. Project Design,
Planning and Programming, Technical Control and
Evaluation. A set of 11 booklets (450 pages)
covering design and construction methods, cost
analysis, site management, operation and
maintenance, work study and incentive schemes.
(International Labour Office, Geneva, n.d.)

V. COUNTRY STUDIES

Abdessatar, Grissa. Agricultural Policies and
Employment: Case Study of Tunisia. (OECD, Paris,
1973)
Andriamananjara, Rajaona. 'Labor Mobilization: The
Moroccan Experience', Center for Research in
Economic Development, Occasional Paper 15
(University of Michigan, Ann Arbor, 1971)
Burki, S. J. 'Interest Group Involvement in West
Pakistan Rural Works Program', Public Policy, vol.
XIX, no. 1, (1971)
Chen, L. C. 'An Analysis of Per Capita Food Grain
Availability in Bangladesh: a Systematic Approach
to Food Planning', The Bangladesh Development
Review, vol. III, no. 2, (1975)
Costa, E. An Assessment of the Flow of Benefits
Generated by Public Investment in the Employment
Guarantee Scheme of Maharashtra. (International
Labour Office, World Employment Programme Working
Paper 2-24/12, Geneva, 1978)
_____. Planning and Organisation of the 'Frentes
de Trabalho' in North-East Brazil. (International
Labour Office, World Employment Programme Working
Paper 2-24/1, Geneva, 1974)

109

Donovan, Graeme. 'Rural Works and Employment: Description and Preliminary Analysis of a Land Army Project in Mysore State, India', Occasional Paper No. 60, Employment and Income Distribution Project, Cornell University

Falcon, W. P., Belinda Dapise and Richard Patten. 'An Experiment in Rural Employment Creation: Indonesia's Kabupaten Program', mimeographed, (1973)

Godbole, Achyug. '"Productive" Relief Works for the Rich', Economic and Political Weekly, Bombay, (28 April, 1973), p.773

Government of Indonesia. Labour Intensive Research in Java and Madura, Manpower Department, Labour Intensive Research Team, mimeographed, (1972)

Government of East Pakistan. Performance Report: Works Programme 1967-68

Government of Pakistan. Evaluation of the People's Works Program, Planning and Development Division, August, (1975)

Guha, S. Organisation, Planning and Administration of the 'Drought-prone Areas Programme' in Ahmednagar and Sholapur Districts of Maharashtra State of India. (International Labour Office, World Employment Programme Working Paper 2-24/4, Geneva, 1975)

_____. Planning, Organisation and Administration of the Rural Employment Guarantee Scheme in Maharashtra State of India. (International Labour Office, World Employment Programme Working Paper 2-24/2, Geneva, 1975)

_____. Policies to Enhance Income Redistributive Potential and Participatory Character of Labour-intensive Rural Public Works Programmes: Some Lessons from the Maharashtra Employment Guarantee Scheme. (International Labour Office, World Employment Working Paper 2-24/16, Geneva, 1979)

Hussain, Syed Mushtag. 'Strategy of Agricultural Development with special reference to Pakistan' (Pakistan Institute of Development Economics, Karachi, mimeographed, 1970)

Institute of Social Studies (New Delhi). Report of the Maharashtra Employment Guarantee Scheme on Women Workers. (International Labour Office, Geneva, 1979)

International Labour Office. 'Roads and Redistribution: A Social Cost-Benefit Study of Labour Intensive Road Construction Methods in Iran', Geneva, (1973)

Kraft, J. D. 'Slum Development in South and Southeast Asia,' paper delivered at the Conference on Town and City Planning, Colombo, (1971).

Lal, Deepak. 'Men and Machines: A Philippines Case Study of Labour-Capital Substitution in Road Construction' (International Labour Office, Geneva, mimeographed, 1973)

Lee, Daniel Kie-Hong. 'National Construction Services: Korea's Experiences in Utilization of Underdeveloped Manpower Resources,' mimeographed, (1969).

Republic of Korea. Ministry of Health and Social Affairs, 'Self Help Work Program', (1968)

Rosser, C. Urbanisation in India, International Urbanisation Survey, (Ford Foundation, New York, n.d.)

Thomas, John W. 'The Rural Works Program and East Pakistan Development', unpublished PhD thesis, Harvard University, 1968

_____. 'The Rural Public Works Programme in East Pakistan', in G. F. Papanek and W. P. Falcon, Development Policy II: The Pakistan Experience (Harvard University Press, Cambridge, 1971)

Phan-Thuy, N. Cost-benefit Analysis of Labour-intensive Public Works Programmes: A Case Study of the 'Travail pour Tous' (TPT) Programme in Mauritius, (International Labour Office, World Employment Programme Working Paper 2-24/3, Geneva, 1975)

_____. Cost-benefit Analysis of Labour-intensive Public Works Programmes: A Case Study of the Pilot-intensive Rural Employment Project (PIREP) in Mangakur Block of Tamil Nadu in India. (International Labour Office, World Employment Programme Working Paper 2-24/10, Geneva, 1978)

_____. National Youth Service Schemes in Sri Lanka: A Survey. (International Labour Office, World Employment Programme Working Paper 2-24/20, Geneva, 1982)

Van der Oever-Pereira, P. Programmes de travaux publics et distribution du temps de travail des femmes: Le cas de Burkina Faso. (International Labour Office, Geneva, 1984)

VI. RECENT SOCIO-ECONOMIC EVALUATIONS OF SPECIFIC COUNTRY PROGRAMMES

The following references are all obtainable from the Emergency Employment Schemes branch of the International Labour Organisation in Geneva.

Bangladesh: Socio-economic Impact Evaluation of the

Special Four-district Rural Works Programme (1985)
Burkina Faso: Evaluation à mi-parcours du programme pilote special de travaux publics (1985)
Dominica Special Works Programmes Related to Reconstruction (1982)
Evaluation of the Nepal Special Public Works Programme (1982)
Evaulation of the Pilot Project for Promotion of Employment and Income Opportunities for Tribal Workers in Bundwan Block, West Bengal, India (1983)
Evaluation of the Tanzania Special Public Works Programme (1983)
Mali: Evaluation finale de programme spécial de travaux publics (1984)
Uganda: Evaluation of the Crash Labour-intensive Employment Programme (1985)